Blessed Are the Meek, the Humble, and the Bold

Memoir of a Remarkable Life Journey

Elsie M. Collins, Ph.D.

iUniverse, Inc.
New York Bloomington

Blessed Are the Meek, the Humble, and the Bold
Memoir of a Remarkable Life Journey

iUniverse books may be ordered through booksellers or by contacting:

iUniverse
1663 Liberty Drive
Bloomington, IN 47403
www.iuniverse.com
1-800-Authors (1-800-288-4677)

ISBN: 978-1-4502-6239-2 (sc)
ISBN: 978-1-4502-6238-5 (dj)
ISBN: 978-1-4502-6237-8 (ebk)

Library of Congress Control Number: 2010914502

Printed in the United States of America

iUniverse rev. date: 11/18/2010

Contents

Prologue

My Foundation

This book is my third. I have now begun to set my sights in several other challenging projects. What sustains me through these projects is what has sustained me all along the way. My life and lifestyle are shaped by selected scriptures from The Holy Bible. Quiet reading and meditating daily give my spirit the sense of wholeness, fullness and direction needed to fill me up spiritually. A few of my favorite readings are listed below.

1. The Lord is My Shepherd and I Shall Not Want. *23rd Psalm*
2. The Ten Commandments. *Exodus 20:1-17*
3. The Beatitudes. *Matthew 5 ch. V.51-48*
4. Let the Words of my Mouth and the Meditations of My Heart, Be Acceptable in Thy Sight, Oh Lord, My Strength and My Redeemer. *Ps.19:14*
5. But I say Unto You – Love Your Enemies, Bless Them That Curse You, Do Good To Them That Hate You, and Pray For Them Which Spitefully Use You and Persecute You. *Matthew 5:43 and 44.*
6. Judge Not That Ye Be Not Judged. *Matthew 7:1.*
7. Ask and It Shall Be Given You. Seek and Ye Shall Find; Knock and It Shall Be Opened Unto You. *Matthew 7:7 and 8.*

8. Blessed is the Man that Walketh Not in the Counsel of the Ungodly, Nor Standeth in the Way of Sinners, Nor Sitteth in the Seat of the Scornful. *Psalm I.*
9. I Will Lift Up Mine Eyes into the Hills From Whence Cometh My Help. My Help Cometh From the Lord. *Psalm 121.*
10. Though I Speak with the Tongues of Men and of Angels and Have Not Love … I am Nothing. *2 Corinthians, 13th chapter.*
11. Praise ye the Lord, Praise God in His Sanctuary, Let Everything that Hath Breath Praise the Lord, Praise Ye the Lord. *Psalm 150.*
12. Bear One Another's Burden, and in This Way You Will Fulfill the Law of Christ. *Gal. 6:2.*
13. If We Are Rich, and See Others in Need, Yet Close Our Hearts Against Them, How can We Claim that We Love God? *1 John 3:17.*
14. God Did Not Give Us a Spirit of Timidity, But a Spirit of Power, of Love, and of Self Discipline. *2 Timothy1:7.*
15. Be Ye Doers of the Word, and Not Hearers Only, Deceiving Your Own Selves. *James 1:22.*
16. He that Dwelleth in the Secret Place of the Most High Shall Abide Under the Shadow of the Almighty. *Psalm 91.*

I enjoy reading, and one of my favorite books is the Bible, probably, the King James' edition. The daily messages from the Upper Room, along with the suggested Biblical readings are basic guides that help me set the tone for living each day. I conclude my readings with a prayer of thanksgiving, praise to God, and a request for His guidance, His care, and that His will be done.

Introduction

I was born almost sixty years after the close of the Civil War. I am the third generation in my family to be born out of slavery. Emzy, my grandfather on my mother's side, was born into slavery in 1856. Emzy's wife, my grandmother, Allie Richardson, was born 1866, a year following the close of the Civil War. However, both Allie's mother Ruthie and her father Hillary Farmer were born into slavery. Emzy's mother, Fillis, and father, Emzy Richardson, Sr., were both slaves and lived on the Vinson plantation in Johnston County, North Carolina.

The system of slavery, which existed in both North and South America, lasted for more than three hundred years. One of the major principles of enslavement was to destroy the positive image the African had of himself and replace it with self-hatred. Self-loathing would make it easy for a slave holding nation to establish and promote white supremacy.

Although some historians occasionally state that Africans were participants in the slave trade, there is very limited evidence to support this theory. The objections to the system were so profound that many captured Africans committed suicide in Africa even before being chained in stalls. Thousands jumped into the oceans while en route to trading posts. Many died after drinking a poisonous mixture they themselves put together after being sold to a slave owner. In-depth historical research suggests that in excess of several million Africans were either murdered or committed suicide because of the cruelty that existed within the American system of slavery. However, millions did survive and were able to live through this cruelty. They are the forerunners of the current African American population in America. I am one of their descendents.

It gives me great pleasure to be one of these descendents, but raises anger in me when I reflect on the pain my forefathers endured to help bring prosperity to America.

African Americans have a deep religious belief system. They rely on a strong connection with a Higher Power, which they believe sustains them. This Higher Power is referred to as God or The Lord, the name used by other Christians in America. However, worship of The Deity by African Americas differs in style and form from that embraced by other Americans. A people living in stress and oppression tend to have a different relationship with The Deity than those who oppress them.

Not many years following the end of the Civil War and the fall of slavery system, a new and different type of human oppression was operative in America. It was the system of segregation and discrimination. I was born into this system and grew up in it.

As a youngster, I had no idea what all that had come before me now meant and the harm it was doing to my self-image and personality. I knew I obeyed the law and carefully followed the instructions of my parents. My ability to live in both sections of the country, north and south, where laws of discrimination and segregation were applied differently, enabled me to make some personal judgments and draw some conclusions that deepened my understanding of the America of opportunity and dreams, as well as its people by individuals' frailties and shortcomings. I made the system work for me. I could not have persevered through all the challenges I faced without strong family values and ties; dedicated teachers in a dedicated school system; continuous religious teaching and guidance; and personal goals, determination, ambition and abilities.

I had my share of ups and downs, pains and pleasures, failures and successes. I was able to find my way through the hard times and trials, rise above them when necessary, and succeed in spite of them. This is my story, abundant with episodes about the people who affected and changed my life and helped formed my identity.

Kissi, That's Me

The neighborhood kids called me Kissi (pronounced Kissy). I was seldom referred to as Elsie, my given name.

They called me a tomboy. I loved being outdoors. I willingly climbed every tree my male playmates sought to conquer. I fished nearby streams and ponds with my grandmother and my distant cousin, Louisa Durham, picked berries and other wild fruits with neighborhood children. My early childhood years, that time when I was known as Kissi, were spent in my grandparents' home in Wilson's Mills, North Carolina.

The name Kissi continues to follow me, much to my delight. Now in my senior years, I will occasionally meet an individual or a relative who greets me with, "Hello, Kissi." To understand who I was then, and who I am today, you have to know something about my grandparents and their offspring.

My Grandparents Allie and Emzy, and Their Offspring

Wilson's Mills, North Carolina

(The Early Years)

The year was 1884, the Civil War had ended almost two decades earlier, and the Southern section of the country remained in ruins. My grandparents, Allie Farmer and Emzy Richardson were in love and, knowing that they would be married soon, very excited. Emzy was a short, stout, man with a copper-toned complexion. His buddies called him "Shorty." Allie was a slender young girl, darker complected than Emzy. Allie was 18 years old and Emzy was 28.

Allie and Emzy did not have economic opportunities awaiting them, which would have enabled them to begin a comfortable life together. They had nothing; but were in the same situation as other Southerners, especially African Americans living in this section of Johnston County in North Carolina. As a matter of fact, all the state's African Americans over the age of 25 had lived in the bondage of slavery and were struggling with the emotional and psychological effects it had had upon their lives. In fact, Emzy, who was affectionately called "Emms," was seven years old when the Civil War ended though Allie was not yet born. Their youth was spent during the period of the Reconstruction of the South. Economically, these were very hard years.

Emms and Allie became husband and wife on a clear, placid day in June 1885. Two years later, on November 24, 1887, their first child was born. They named him Dominion Purl. Everyone called him Purl or D.P.. Allie was 21 years old at the time, and Emms was 31.

This loving couple had planned on a larger family. Allie became pregnant again in 1889. Ellen Mitchener, the mid-wife, and also Allie's aunt, moved in with them to watch Allie because she was beginning to have some problems early in her pregnancy. The problems continued and resulted in a miscarriage.

The couple was expecting another child in 1891. However, after a few months into her pregnancy, Allie began to cramp and bleed. She lost the baby.

At the age of 27 in 1893, Allie again discovered that she was pregnant. After a few months, Aunt Ellen again moved in. Unfortunately, however, after a few months, Allie again began to cramp and bleed. It was a third miscarriage.

Persistent in their efforts to build their family, in 1896, Allie gave birth to their second child. She was a baby girl and they named her Ruth Lucille. Purl was at the time eleven years old. Emms was beside himself with pride for this is really what he felt was missing in his life; a baby girl. Aunt Ellen had moved in with the Richardsons when Allie learned she was pregnant, and remained the entire nine months. Allie was able to stay off her feet and get extra rest as needed. It seems to have paid off.

Allie and Emms had two more children and no more miscarriages. Another son was born in 1899. They named him Willis David. The fourth and last child was born in 1901: another daughter, Nellie.

Allie and Emms were fully aware of the lack of opportunities in education for their children. Neither Southern states nor border-states provided public education for African American children. If there were schools or opportunities for growth and development in education, they were provided by philanthropists or foundations, but not by public funds.

Despite limited education opportunities in the late 19th century, Allie had learned to read as did her four sisters – Julia, Arkannie, Rachel and Nora. It is quite possible that they received help from a former slave owner. Emms never did learn how to read. It was Allie's pleasure and responsibility to read the Bible aloud to him daily and the *Raleigh Times* newspaper on the weekend.

Emms was known to be a strong father figure, and carefully supervised the activities of his children. He was especially stern with Ruth, his oldest daughter.

When their children were young, Allie and Emms made sure that their children attended the one- and two-room county school provided for "colored" children. When Ruth completed the grades in the nearby schools, she was sent to Raleigh to attend St. Augustine High School and College. Here she completed an accredited high school curriculum. She remained at St. Augustine and completed the normal school Teacher Education Program and graduated as a teacher of elementary education. It was a glorious day when young Ruth was hired by the Board of Education of the City of Raleigh and subsequently by the Durham, North Carolina school district. She proudly taught at elementary school districts in rural sections of both these cities.

A young teacher by the name of Sallie A. Grady came to Wilson's Mills to teach in the colored elementary school. It was the custom, in those days, for teachers to live in the homes of the citizens of the town and provisions were made by the school district to take care of this concern. Miss Sally was fortunate enough to find a room at the home of "Miss Allie" and Mr. Emms Richardson. During this period of time, she and Purl fell in love and eventually got married.

Purl had completed his schooling at the local two-room school and was now working full-time at the Wilson's Mills (lumber mills for which the town was named). His ambition was to go to Kittrell College in Kittrell, North Carolina and study ministry. In 1918, he graduated from Kittrell as an African Methodist Episcopal minister.

Younger son, David did not wish to go away to school. He chose to stay close to home and his Momma. The younger Richardson daughter, Nellie, was epileptic. She finished the nearby schools, but stayed close to home to be watched over and cared for by her parents. A local resident taught her to sew and she became an excellent seamstress.

Aunt Ellen delivered a baby boy for a woman in the Purifoy family. This delivery left the mother quite weak and unable to care for her infant son. The father and Aunt Ellen had to make an important decision immediately concerning the well-being of the baby. The best decision they could make, they felt at that time, was for Aunt Ellen to take the baby home with her. Meanwhile, other decisions could be made for the baby if necessary. Aunt Ellen was 60 years old at this time of her life. Her husband had passed away only three years earlier. Since then, she had set up temporary lodging in the home of her niece, Allie, and her family. However, since she was a midwife she spent a great deal of her time traveling, living in the home of expectant mothers, delivering babies and caring for both the mother and the baby for a period of time, following the delivery. Aunt Ellen was the best known midwife around, and she came to the aid of both white and "colored" mothers.

The year was 1910, and it was a warm summer evening in June when Aunt Ellen arrived home with the infant. When she explained to Allie and Emms the critical circumstances at (this) home of the infant, they understood and were sympathetic. They called the baby infant Leamon, and he became a permanent member of the Richardson family. Thereafter, he was known as the baby brother.

Ruth, Allie's daughter, was a very popular girl. Besides having a few beaux, Ruth, like other young women, was also interested in advancing herself, so she took a teaching job in the County of Durham where she received more money. It was during this time she met a young man by the name of Charlie McIntosh, who had recently moved to Durham from Laurinburg, North Carolina. A very serious courtship developed, they fell in love and were soon married.

Ruth and Charlie made a home together in Durham, and Ruth gave birth to four daughters – me, Allie (named after our grandmother), Elizabeth, and Nellie (named after her Aunt Nellie). I was the first born.

Because of complications surrounding the birth of Nellie, she was born at Ruth's parents' home in Wilson's Mills. The three eldest daughters were born in the hospital in Durham. Baby Nellie was a sickly child and her health continued to deteriorate until her death around 1929.

Following the death of baby Nellie, Ruth returned to Durham and took baby Elizabeth with her. She left my sister Allie and me in Wilson's

Mills to spend a few more months with her parents. I was about five or six years old at the time.

Emms, my grandfather, I was often told, was very pleased to have the girls stay with them. He really wanted to keep them always, but their parents would not move them permanently.

A Close Call

Being the first grandchild, and the first child of his eldest daughter (born after a series of miscarriages), meant that I was special in the eyes of my grandfather. I remember sitting in his lap a lot and being held by him. Even when he was quite ill and I was in school, he welcomed me into his lap to read him a story (he never went to school, nor did he learn to read).

Several times during the year, my grandmother Allie would go to Durham to get me, keep me in Wilson's Mills for a few months and then return me to my parents in Durham. Because my parents had to work, they had to hire a baby sitter when I was not with my grandparents in Wilson's Mills.

As a young adult I found out from my mother that, when I was about 2 or 3 years old, something happened that shook the family thoroughly. My mother took me to the babysitter on her way to school, as was the custom. It was my dad's responsibility to pick me up as he came home from work first. However, on one particular afternoon when he arrived at the home of the babysitter, he was met at the door by one of the adults. This adult told my dad that his wife had not left me with them that morning and further, the sitter had no idea where my mom had taken me. Dad was dumbfounded and attempted to enter the home to talk with other adults there about their little Elsie. However, he was blocked and asked to leave in the wake of heated remarks.

Charlie immediately ran and called his wife and detailed the situation. He asked her if she was sure that she had dropped me off at the usual babysitting home. This news sent my mom in a panic and she quickly joined her husband at the babysitter's home. The same denial response from the babysitter continued and my parents were again prevented from entering the home. Family members, friends, as well as the police were contacted. A screaming and shouting match ensued and it soon drew a crowd in front of the home. When the police arrived with

Charlie, they were finally able to enter the home. There they found me. I am told that when mom picked me up, I was limp, drowsy and non-responsive. My parents were quite frightened. With police assistance, they took me to the hospital immediately. After a necessary stay in the hospital, which lasted a few weeks, I was out of danger and on the way to good health.

What happened to me in the house that day – whether I was dropped, drugged, abused, or all of the above – I will never fully know.

Following this near-fatal incident, understandably, my parents became very skeptical of babysitters and began to depend more and more upon my grandparents in Wilson's Mills. Parental visits, which occurred about twice per month, were arranged. I recall short visits to Durham and my parents made brief visits to Wilson's Mills.

Eventually, my grandparents became the principal babysitter of all three of their granddaughters.

This arrangement continued throughout our formative years of growth and development. Because my mom was a teacher, she was at home during the summer recess. So early in May, my grandmother, Allie, brought my sisters and me to Durham to spend the summer with our parents. Grandpa Richardson didn't want me to spend the whole summer away from him, so my grandma usually came and got me before vacation time was over.

I came from a close-knit family which prides itself on what it can create and pass on to the next generation. My grandfather was one of three cousins (Lorenzo and Oscar Vinson, being the other two cousins) who jointly purchased adjoining properties totaling several acres on a busy road in Wilson's Mills. Each cousin built a family home. Cousins Emms and Oscar had enough frontage to also build a second home for their sons. Emms built a home for his son Purl and his wife Sally, and later Oscar built a home for his son Herbert and his wife Ada. This was between 1910 and 1920. These homes began as small three-room houses, just big enough to accommodate a small, but growing family. By 1930, just before my grandfather's death in 1933, my grandparents' home had grown to five rooms with an enclosed side-back porch, plus a large decorative front porch.

The Influence of My Extended Family North Carolina

(Durham, The Later Years)

Substantial changes in the economic level and family structure of the McIntosh family were about to take place. I was already spending most of my time with my grandparents in Wilson's Mills and making periodic visits to Durham to see my parents. Because of an unfortunate incident with the babysitter, this arrangement had to be made. Allie and Elizabeth's life style was just the opposite for they lived at home in Durham with our parents. My mother, Ruth, was successful as an elementary school teacher of colored children in a Durham County rural school. My dad, Charlie, because of his color and the fact that he lacked proper educational preparation, was only able to get low-paying manual jobs. On many occasions, he served as babysitter for his children. Our family did well, however, and was able to maintain a middle-class economic status.

Uncle Purl and Aunt Sally

My Uncle Purl, who stood about 5'10" tall, had dark brown skin, and weighed about 160 pounds, became a very successful and somewhat prominent minister in the African Methodist Episcopal Church. He served as minister in several up-and-coming churches in Eastern North

Carolina. His wife, Sally, a Mulatto, was considered an effective teacher in the elementary colored schools in Johnston County. She was later honored by the county for having spent 50 years as an educator in the public school system.

Purl was considered an outstanding preacher. People would travel far to hear him preach. He was also well regarded in the conference of the AME Church. High officials such as the Presiding Elder and the Bishop of the conference often met at his home to confer and even to spend a few days. Sometimes, on these occasions, I being the oldest of the grandchildren, was called over to my Aunt and Uncle's home to help out. I would set the table, or wash dishes, help make up the beds, dust the furniture and so on. I didn't mind, for I enjoyed listening to those adults, church leaders, teachers, etc., talk about their business and experiences.

Purl and Sally had a very fancy home. The basic floor plan was Victorian with a wide hall that began at the front door and ran through the house to an enclosed back porch. Off the right of this hall were a large guest bedroom, a smaller guest bedroom, and there own bedroom. To the left was a well-furnished living room. Going through the living room one would enter a well-furnished dining room, which led to a rather large kitchen. The kitchen's second door led to the back enclosed porch. At the right end of the porch was a large comfortable bathroom/dressing room combination. A large semi-curved front porch decorated the front of the house. The porch had four large columns with a brick foundation about three feet high. Facing the house to the right, before reaching his parents home was a driveway for his car. He could also drive the car the length of this home into a completed single-car garage. There was a large, fenced-in backyard where his chickens roamed about, but often found a way to get into the vegetable garden of about an acre that he shared with his parents next door.

Probably because Purl was so much older than his siblings, they respected him and listened to him during their growing-up years. Allie and Emms, my grandparents, required the children to refer to him as Brother Purl and his wife as Sister Sally. These names were often shortened to Bro Purl and Sis Sally.

Sally grew up in a community of light-skinned people of mixed descent. Some members of her family, however, especially her sisters

Rena and Minnie came to visit her in Wilson's Mills once in a while. However, when Sally and Purl went to visit family in her home town of Dudley, her husband usually would not come along. Often, he would leave her there and pick her up later.

Sally and Purl did not have any children of their own. However, circumstances beyond their control made them parents anyway. Thomas Grady's second wife passed away, leaving five young children. His first wife, Sis Sally's mother, had also passed away, but her children, including Sis Sally, were either grown, independent, or married. The children from the second marriage needed care and it became the responsibility of the older siblings to take on this responsibility. Luetta was the youngest of these children and she was under five years old. When decisions were made regarding the placement of these children, Luetta was placed in the home of Sally and Purl. She went to live in Wilson's Mills, there she remained and grew up. She received the best education available. After completing the public elementary school in Wilson's Mills, she went to the prep high schools at St. Augustine College in Raleigh. After completing high school there, she enrolled in St. Augustine College and completed her degree in elementary education. Her future husband, Maxwell Virgel, matriculated at St. Augustine College following his tour of duty in World War II. Luetta and Max were married and moved to Long Island City, New York. They had two daughters, Cheryl and Maxine. Maxwell went to work for the City of New York, and Luetta went to work in a day care facility. Years later, the family opened their own day care business. Their business flourished and became quite a success, employing Luetta and Maxine.

Sis Sally enjoyed fifty years of successful teaching, but by the time she was in her mid-seventies, her health had begun to deteriorate. She seemed quite nervous and worried most of the time. At a time when Purl was not at home, her brothers came and convinced her to go with them. They registered her in a hospital in Goldshore, where she stayed until her death July 2, 1974. Purl could only visit his wife, but could not bring her home. He had a stroke in 1972, and died November 24, 1974. They were married 64 years. He was 87 years old and she was 89 when they passed away.

Leamon Grows Up

Among the people who had continuing influence in my life was my Uncle Leamon (Lee).

Leamon, the baby boy that Aunt Ellen brought to my grandparents' (Allie and Emzy) home to raise, was growing up. It was now about the mid 1920s (1926 or 1927), and Leamon was about sixteen years old. He had completed all of the eight grades offered at the colored elementary school, but did not wish to continue his education at the high school in Smithfield. So he busied himself doing odd jobs about town. The town's mill operations ceased in 1925.

Leamon was a big youngster for his age; he was tall, big boned and handsome. This physique made him a big hit among the young ladies of the community, especially the young teachers.

But Leamon was getting restless. The town was getting too small for him. With his parents' permission, he wrote to his sister, Ruth, in Durham, and asked if he could come and live with her and Charlie. Permission was granted, so Leamon left his Wilson's Mills home and moved to Durham to live with his sister.

There in this home, Leamon completed his growing up years. He took classes evenings and on weekends in industrial arts and machine shop. With these learned skills he was able to maintain steady employment.

By the time he reached his late twenties, Leamon was progressing rather well. But his sister Ruth and her family had moved to the City of New York.

With his sister Ruth living in New York, Leamon, also known as "Lee," got the desire to go North. He also knew relatives and friends who were living in the City of Philadelphia. So Leamon decided to move to Philadelphia with the help of family and friends and soon found very good jobs.

After a few years, he met his soul mate, Anna. Anna was a mature woman who had divorced an abusive husband and was now raising her young daughter. She was a hard worker and a good homemaker. She and Lee were a good match, so after a couple of years of courtship, they married.

Anna and Lee made many fine friends during the years they lived in Philadelphia. And members of the influential Griffin family were among them. However, it was members of this family who encouraged

Anna and Lee to make an investment in real estate at Wildwood, New Jersey. They took advantage of a very good situation and purchased two homes. One was a building with two completed apartments, and the other was a small house adjacent to the apartments.

Lee and Anna decided to leave Philadelphia and move into one of their apartments in Wildwood, New Jersey. This was the late 1960's.

Lee had landed a very good job working for the State of New Jersey. He was a father figure and house counselor for troubled teenage boys living in cottages assigned by the State of New Jersey. His move to Wildwood did not jeopardize his job, for he was assigned eventually, to a similar position closer to Wildwood.

Anna worked as a domestic. The family she worked for in Philadelphia also had another home in Wildwood. Some family member lived in it all year round. Anna worked for this family close to forty years. They were instrumental in helping Lee and Anna furnish their homes and get settled in Wildwood. Upon the death of a matriarch of this Wildwood family, many fine antiques were given to Anna, including a large organ for her home. She and Lee gave it to her church in Wildwood.

My young daughters and I were living in Trenton, New Jersey when Uncle Lee and Aunt Anna were living in Wildwood. We kept in close contact with them, as we did other members of our family. Lee and Anna often came to Trenton to visit the girls and me. But a special vacation for the girls was when I drove down to Wildwood and spent a week with Aunt Anna and Uncle Lee. This usually occurred during spring break, when the beaches were not too crowded nor the sun too hot. I drove the 125 miles one way to Wildwood.

By the late 1980's, Lee's diabetes was out of control and he passed away in 1986. Anna's only daughter took over management of the property. She disassociated her mother with members of Lee's family by changing the telephone number and refusing to answer all mail. Contact with Aunt Anna was lost.

Brother David

David was not interested in furthering his education, as did his older brother Purl, and older sister, Ruth. He was content completing his education in the local two-room school where Miss Sally, Miss Mamie Grandy and Miss Lottie Holt taught. He picked up local jobs in the

Wilson's Mills, on cotton or tobacco farms and helped his father, Mr. Emms, on odd jobs.

David was considered a rather good-looking, average sized man with dark brown skin. He was very popular among the women, but it seems he never loved anyone well enough to marry her.

He was sometimes looked upon as a Mama's boy, being the baby son. He usually worked nearby and stayed at home with his parents. His nieces were very fond of him and he often played with them, especially little Elsie.

In his youth, about age twenty, David developed a serious drinking problem and was considered an alcoholic by the time he was in his mid-twenties. However, he never let alcohol interfere with his job responsibilities. He would work diligently on his job during the week, but allowed himself to become limp with alcohol from Friday night until Sunday afternoon. By Sunday night he was sober and ready for work on Monday morning.

During the hours he was in a drunken stupor, he would lose all of his money – that is, the money he had earned during the week – and find himself broke on Sunday night. There were times when he would pass out on the street or in someone's home. A member of the family was summoned to come and get him. I was the child who went, for it seemed he would not listen to anyone, but me. I cannot remember what technique I used to get him to obey, but being a child about 10-11 years old, I would talk to him as normally and naturally as I did each day, such as "Brother, let's go home now," or "Brother, it's time to eat. Your food is on the table; come let's go home." He always said, "My nephew has come down from New York to take me home." When he said "nephew" everyone knew he was drunk.

David became custodian for a small rural school in Johnston County in 1943. The job also provided a small house in which he was to live while carrying out his responsibilities. David lived in the house, but came home to his mother's home on the weekend. There was a weekend when David did not come home, so his cousins and buddies decided to go to his home in the country to find out why. When they arrived, they found David sitting on his porch leaning back against a porch pillar. They ran to him calling his name, but he did not answer. When they approached him, they found out why. David was dead. The year was 1946 and David was 46 years old.

Aunt Nellie

Aunt Nellie, called "Aunt Nell" by us children, was very interested in school. She had a hunger and a thirst to learn. But Nellie was epileptic; therefore, she was limited in mobility and the ability to get around. Her parents, (my grandparents) Emzy and Allie Richardson, simply would not allow her to go far without their presence.

Therefore, Nellie's formal education was limited to the offerings of the two-room school nearby. The teachers, Miss Sally (who later married Nellie's brother Purl), Miss Mamie Grandy, and Mrs. Lottie Holt, were members of the local community and knew Nellie's epileptic condition. Still, her parents were afraid to take a chance with this condition by sending her away to school. Nellie learned all she could from the local school, but did not go away to further her education. Her relatives and other local friends taught her how to sew and she became a first-rate seamstress. She made some of the fancy dresses that my sisters and I wore as babies and small children.

When Nellie was in her early twenties, she became fascinated with a minister who was twice her age. His name was Reverend Green. Nellie ran away from home, married Rev. Green and went to Wilmington, North Carolina to live. Her parents were devastated, especially her father. After a few months of bliss and fun, the marriage fell on hard times. Reverend Green saw Nellie as someone he had the duty to discipline, so he began to beat her. When this news reached Nellie's family, her mother and father went to Wilmington to get her. They successfully brought her home. By this time, she was also sick and so was Reverend Green. Thereafter, Nellie was unable to spend much time with her husband. Eventually, he became quite ill and passed away. Nellie never returned to Wilmington to live again.

Nellie remained a widow for several years, but she was always a flirt and had several boyfriends. In the early 1960's, she married her second husband, who was also old enough to be her father. His name was Fenner "Dit" Rogers. Nellie was also Mr. Dit's second wife. He, his wife and children had lived in a northern state for many years. After his wife died, his children were grown and married, Mr. Dit returned home to Wilson's Mills to live near his sisters Ora and Fannie Vinson. When he married Nellie, he moved into her parents' home with her. Nellie became unable to care for herself, so her Brother Purl put her in a nursing home facility in Goldsboro, North Carolina. She died in 1965 at age 64. Uncle Dit passed away in 1968 at age 93.

My Early Years: Short Journey

When I reached the legal age to enter school, I was enrolled in the primer (equivalent of today's kindergarten) of the Wilson's Mills Elementary School for Colored Students. I was a quiet child of dark brown complexion. I had long black hair, which was kept braided in three or four braids. My quiet, timid appearance gave the impression that I was easy prey for those who wished to beat me up. This appearance evidently carried into the classroom, for an incident occurred earlier in second grade that upset the members of my family. Without resolution, my family withdrew me from the school and sent me to Short Journey Elementary School for Colored Students.

At Short Journey, I received an excellent elementary education for the next six years. I traveled to school each day with two teachers, Mrs. Rochelle Vinson, the fourth grade and music teacher, and her daughter Miss Ione Vinson, the second grade teacher. This meant that I spent most of my entire elementary school years in the company of teachers. I remained with the Vinson family after school for special meetings, and at night to attend meetings and programs. Since I was a respectful and obedient child, the Vinson's had no problem leaving me for short periods of time with school parents and friends when necessary.

Before graduating from the elementary grades all students in the upper middle grades in the state must take and pass the National Academic Achievement Test. The test was administered when I was in seventh grade.

After the tests were corrected and the grades distributed to the various school districts, the Johnston County School District received some very interesting news. Four students from the colored school, Short Journey, had scored exceptionally high; even higher than white students in that county. This news was quite disturbing to the county superintendent of schools, Mr. Marrow. Mr. Marrow was urged by the School Board of Education to get to the bottom of the "problem." Mr.

Marrow contacted and met with Mrs. Cooper, Principal of the Short Journey Elementary School for Colored Students about this problem. He also met with the four little girls who had scored so high on the test. I was one of the little girls. The other three were Martha Williams, Annie Mae Penny, and Edith Sanders. Martha Williams made the highest score, Annie Mae Penny came second and I was third. I was told that all four scores were very close; a difference of one or two points. I recall my meeting with the Superintendent of Schools, the many questions he asked about my parents, and about the teachers who administered the tests at Short Journey.

During those years a Fulbright Scholarship was available to those students who excelled on tests, as well as academically. During those years, also, the laws of segregation and discrimination were firmly in place. This meant that the opportunity to receive this scholarship was extended to white students only. It was the belief that non-white, African American students did not have the mental capacity to excel academically. Therefore, such a scholarship was not extended to us.

My colleagues and I at Short Journey were too young to fight for our rights. However, our teachers at Short Journey did fight, but their hands were tied and the battle was lost before it began.

Living With the Fews

Back in Durham, my parents got some very exciting news. One of their friends told them that Mrs. William Preston Few, the wife of the President of Duke University, was looking for an individual who would serve as "housekeeper of the President's Mansion" on the university campus. The salary was very good. As a matter of fact, it was much greater than that which my mother was receiving as a teacher. After discussing it with my father, mom decided to seek the job. Upon being interviewed, she was immediately hired for the position.

The President's mansion was a very large, two-story red brick home. It had many rooms, an attic and a finished basement. It was set in the center of a large garden of flowering plants, tropical plants, exotic and rare trees, shrubs, hedges and vines. In this home lived Dr. William Preston Few, his wife and five sons. The sons were William, Lyne, Kendrick, Randolph and Yancy Preston. The Few's oldest sons were students either at the University or juniors or seniors in high school near the university.

Preston, the youngest son, was ill with an incurable palsy. This condition made it difficult for him to walk and to talk clearly. Therefore, he went to a special school and was picked up daily by a driver.

Ruth accepted a job which involved a great deal of responsibility. Her job was a kind of managerial one, although it may not have been considered as such at that time. The chief yard man, the maid, and the butler/chauffer reported and communicated daily with my mother. She kept records and communicated daily with Mrs. Few. Workers were paid by Mrs. Few. In addition to her managerial responsibilities, my mother also prepared all meals – breakfast, lunch and dinner, assisted by the butler, who served them.

Dr. Few was a very busy man. His many responsibilities as head of a large, growing university included arranging and hosting conferences, meetings, luncheons and dinners. Many of these gatherings were held at his home, sometimes on a weekly basis. If those in attendance did not exceed an agreed upon number that the family had established, my mom, the butler and a few other helpers mom knew would handle the cooking and service for the occasion. However, if the occasion became a large one with several people, a catering service was engaged to accommodate the special crowd.

Mom's new job also brought on a change for our family housing situation. My parents were asked to move from their home on Roxboro Street to the two-bedroom apartment over the garage at the President's mansion.

My parents' child care situation, likewise, changed. I was already spending more time with my grandparents than my two sisters. This move meant that all three of us spent more time during the school year with our grandparents in Wilson's Mills, and spent the summer months, June through August, with our parents at Duke. Looking back, we didn't view our situation as unusual although I am sure many of our contemporaries were not required to be so mobile and upscale.

Preston Few and I were both the same age. So we became playmates. We rode our tricycles, roller-skated, and played catch together. We ten-year-olds were fast friends. Preston passed away six years later, after our family had moved to New York City.

My mother's position as housekeeper at the President's mansion went well. Her salary was almost doubled and her children's well-being was secure. But my dad did not have a steady job. My mom made it her objective to get him a job. Dad was subsequently hired as part-time gardener and full-time handyman by Mrs. Few. Now, the entire family lived and worked at the President's mansion on the campus of Duke University.

My mother had many memorable experiences as housekeeper for the President of Duke University, but one of the most thrilling was the time where the President of the United States, Franklin Delano

Roosevelt and his wife Eleanor were guests of the Fews. The evening of the banquet meant extensive, in-depth planning by my mom and Mrs. Few. This included a guest list of carefully selected friends and dignitaries; a very tight security system; and a menu to excite the taste buds of everyone. Mrs. Few sought mom's input when appropriate, but my mother had her own plan for the help needed to assist her and the butler in food preparation and serving. My mother contacted the helpers she had in mind and gave an extensive explanation of the upcoming occasion when she would need their help. They were all excited and in agreement with the terms offered. These helpers were my grandmother and my grandmother's sister, Arkannie Farmer, both of Wilson's Mills, plus my dad, who was already serving as a handyman. After necessary background checks and questioning, mom's family members were approved by security and banquet preparations were on.

The evening of the banquet was a huge success. The house was alive with governmental officials, and dignitaries in education, business, and industry. My manager mom and her support system apparently handled the occasion with utmost sophistication. My mother's abilities as a good teacher no doubt kept her in good stead.

In the early 1930's, my mother lost three very important members of her family. At the age of 90, her grandmother's sister, Ellen, fell in a nearby field as she returned from visiting family members. She died immediately following the fall. Mom's father, Emzy, passed away in 1932 as the result of a serious heart condition. He was 75 years old. The next year, 1933, her grandmother, Ruthie Farmer, passed away of old age it was believed. She was 104 years old.

The McIntoshes Move to Jamaica, New York

My mother had many relatives and friends who were living in New York, and they were constantly encouraging her to leave the South and bring our family to New York City. Here there promised to be better paying jobs. Also, it was well known that the North offered black Americans more freedom of self-expression and more opportunities to leverage their talents with less fear of being put down, or worse, lynched.

My parents often discussed this idea, but made no decision to move, until the mid 1930's.

My father left Durham around 1935 for New York. In Jamaica, New York with a friend, he shared a rental house. He sent for my mother in 1936. As they established their home and looked for work, they discovered that the only work available to them was low-paying domestic jobs. Both of my parents found work in this capacity.

My sister and I spent the summer months with our parents in New York City, but returned to our grandparents' home in Wilson's Mills in September to attend school. Each year, when school closed in May, Allie and I traveled to New York to spend the summer months with our parents.

My sister Allie was entering adolescence at this time, maturing physically. By this time, my grandmother was having difficulty making her obey. Family members suggested that Allie should be sent to New York to live with our parents, where she would be supervised by our father. So, at the close of the fifth year of school at the Wilson's Mills Elementary School for Colored Students, Allie went to Jamaica, N.Y.

to live with our parents. She never again lived in the south. Elizabeth and I remained in Wilson's Mills with our grandmother and visited our parents when school closed each year.

Though we as youngsters were unaware of it, my mother and father had already begun to drift apart in the late 1930's. By the early 1940's, my father had left our home in Jamaica and moved to Harlem with his girlfriend, Charlotte, and her daughter. My mother had enrolled Allie in the Jamaica school system, but Allie was often truant from school. Allie was a tall, big child for her age, and therefore had been able to escape truant officers by carrying herself as a young adult. This forced our mother to constantly give excuses why Allie was not in school. My mother and Allie, who was then thirteen, also moved to Harlem, and shared an apartment with my mother's cousin, Jessie Vinson, and her boyfriend. This couple was very influential in Allie's life, for she respected the authority of the male of the household and began to settle down. Allie was withdrawn from the Jamaica school system. Her truancy ended when we moved to Harlem.

My mother had difficulty finding work that would provide her with a decent income. Her degree in elementary education and her experiences in management and the culinary arts were not considered adequate for employment by the New York City Board of Education. Graduates from Southern schools were not considered on par with graduates from Northern schools, especially New York City Schools. Also, a master's degree, and passage of an examination, were required to teach in New York City. My mother had two years of college-level courses required for teaching at that time in the South. It was apparent that America's age-old system of discrimination was found in New York in a different version. Because of prevailing attitudes, she was forced to seek work outside of the teaching profession. She had to run around from place to place, filling out applications. After facing various rejections, my mother accepted a job as a chamber maid at the Hotel Lincoln in mid-town Manhattan.

Allie, reaching the ripe age of 17, began to take a more cooperative attitude. She found a job with decent pay that she would stick with for a few years. This was a sleep-in job with a family named Jacobs.

Part of Allie's personal support system was a friend of hers named Ida Pettis. Ida was also a maid and she worked for a family in the same vicinity. Ida and her husband, John, were happily married with one young son, whom they called Pee Wee. John was a college graduate who had just recently landed a substantial job with the City of New York. They became quite influential in Allie's life and the decisions she began to make for herself. Our families became closely attached.

No doubt, my mother's teenage girls were a handful, but we respected her and, with few exceptions, obeyed her. Looking back, I would say she was consistent in her demands of her daughters, but not demanding. We had some neighborhood friends, but we visited with them on the stoop or in the small park across the street. Mother did not allow us to freely visit the homes of neighbors or friends as was the Southern custom. And neighbors and friends did not visit our home. In the big city, when we went out socializing on our own, my mother required that there be at least two sisters together.

Another jarring incident struck the family in August 1943. It was my mother's custom to spend the month of August at the home of her mother in Wilson's Mills. We daughters stayed at home in New York. This particular time, Daddy's sister, Aunt Alice, called us to say that our father was extremely ill in Harlem Hospital. She said if we wanted to see him alive we should go to the hospital immediately. We called our mother and gave her the message. She told us what to do. When we got to the hospital to visit Dad, we had to be escorted to his room by an adult because we were too young and small. When he passed away, we contacted the Delaney Funeral Home on Seventh Avenue as instructed by our mom. Mr. Delaney, in turn, contacted our mother in Wilson's Mills, and all arrangements were made for the funeral, which was to be held in Wilson's Mills. The funeral director purchased the ticket for our father, but Allie and I purchased our own ticket. Elizabeth was already in the south because she was still in school in 1943. Allie and I accompanied our father's body to the South. I vaguely remember this sad time, but felt some sense of detachment as we hadn't seen much of our dad during our adolescent years, and I had been very preoccupied with working my way through college. The funeral was held at the Union Hill AME Church and he is buried in the family plot. He was 43 years old.

Cousin Charlotte Moves to New York

My mother's first cousin, Charlotte Wilder, graduated from the Johnston County Training School in the early 1940's. Although Charlotte had a male cousin, John M. Wilder, and a brother, Marilyn Wilder living in White Plains, New York, Charlotte's parents, Nora and Major Wilder, decided to send her to live with my mom and us in New York City. So Charlotte moved from Wilson's Mills to Harlem to live with us in the mid 1940's. She soon got a job and was able to help support herself.

Charlotte became a part of the team when the girls went out to socialize. Charlotte was one year older than Allie, and almost a year younger than I. As a teenager and young adult, she fit in nicely, for the girls got along as sisters, with my mother as the parent.

When Charlotte chose to become a nurse, she enrolled in Harlem School of Nursing at Harlem Hospital toward a career as a Licensed Practical Nurse (LPN). She later graduated with all the necessary credentials, and went to work in the city hospitals and health systems.

Charlotte later fell in love with a young man named Murph. When she told my mother that she wanted to get married, the home was prepared for the marriage, with the cousin's participating. Charlotte and Murph were married in mom's home and they got themselves an apartment uptown.

During the 1950's, my mother also served as parent to another child. This was Little Ruth, the daughter of Margaret Boylan. Little Ruth was also a cousin. She is the granddaughter of my mother's first cousin, Melissa Boylan.

When Elizabeth was in high school in Wilson's Mills, Little Ruth spent more time with her than she did her mother, Margaret. Elizabeth became very attached to Little Ruth and usually carried her around. Little Ruth had a maladjusted eye and Elizabeth wanted to bring her to New York for corrective surgery. She was successful in having one phase of the surgery done. Little Ruth stayed with the girls at home during her recovery. However, Margaret would not allow a second phase of surgery to be done, so Little Ruth had to return to Wilson's Mills.

My mother began to show signs of ill health in the late 1940's. However, she made every effort to hide it from my sisters and me. All three of us, though young, had selected career goals and were now in pursuit of them. I was doing an excellent job as social studies teacher at the Booker T. Washington Junior High School in Dover, Delaware. I was also sharing my small income with my mother. Once every month I would spend a weekend at home in New York with my mother and, of course, spent the entire summer at home.

This year, 1950, my mother was definitely going to retire. My sisters and I had been after her to do so for a few years now. She finally decided to take our advice. My mother went to Wilson's Mills the first week of August, as was the custom. Elizabeth had gone south on business in July, but decided to remain until August so that she could spend some quality time with our mother before returning to New York.

On the morning of August 25, 1950, about 7:00 a.m. Elizabeth, who was sleeping with my mother, heard strange noises coming from her. Elizabeth got up and began to shake and call her, but she did not respond. Elizabeth called her grandmother who came into the room immediately. They both called and shook her, but she did not respond. She had died in her sleep.

My Sisters Allie and Elizabeth, and I, Become Young Adults

I had graduated from Johnston County Training School with highest honors, which made me valedictorian of my class. In fact, I received many honors and awards for my achievements, and special interests while in high school, as well as a four-year, paid scholarship to Bennett College in Greensboro, North Carolina. At my mother's urging, I did not accept the four-year scholarship to Bennett College, but went, instead, to Kittrell College in Kittrell, North Carolina.

Kittrell was a small four-year Methodist college, established by the A.M.E. conference and supported mainly by the conference, philanthropists and student fees. The student population was small. It consisted of many young, black males who were studying for the ministry; several students who were young adults; and some who were married. A small share of the students were young women and a small number of students were fresh out of high school. I was one of the students right out of high school.

I am convinced that my uncle, Rev. Purl Richardson, was quite influential in persuading my mother to send me to Kittrell rather than to Bennett, because he had graduated from Kittrell.

I spent two years at Kittrell, but withdrew from my studies mainly due to the lack of funds and the need to help provide financial support to my mother in New York. Elizabeth, who was about five years behind me, was still in high school at the Johnston County Training School in Smithfield. She continued to live with our grandparents in Wilson's Mills during the school year, just as I had done. By the late 1940's, she was out of high school and had come to New York to join her mother and sisters, Allie and me.

Allie grew out of her rebellious years and began to advance her education. She earned a degree as a Licensed Practical Nurse and was gainfully employed in the New York City Health System.

Sibling rivalry became a problem between Allie and Elizabeth at home. So Elizabeth moved out and got herself an apartment in the 300 block of 138th Street. It was located in the building where our cousins Martha and Louise Vinson lived. These two adults looked after Elizabeth.

Catering, Elizabeth's (Lizzy's) Passion

Mother approached Lizzy about college once she was out of high school. Although Lizzy had not definitely chosen a career, she was sure it was not going to be teaching. Her mother had been a teacher and now I was pursuing that profession. Lizzy, however, wanted no part of a teaching career.

Cooking was Lizzy's joy. She enjoyed experimenting with types of dishes – making this and omitting that, then waiting for the results and enjoying the surprises and questions. She showed plenty of talent setting tables with decorative napkins, table cloths and silverware and then adding the final touch with bouquets of flowing colors of flowers. Lizzy worked as a chamber maid with our mother, at a mid-town hotel, while she also started her own catering service. She began to make contacts with other caterers. Elizabeth's talents were soon recognized and appreciated by her family members.

Lizzy eventually took a giant step into small business by accepting small catering engagements in New York City. Her name and fame slowly took hold. Her cousin Martha, and a friend by the name of Roberta, were hired. Allie, Roberta and I usually worked as waitresses and clean-up crew when needed. I was one of the waitresses for Elizabeth when she catered a very special gathering for a tin industry tycoon at Sutton Place South, New York City. This tin industry tycoon periodically employed Elizabeth at his Midtown apartments for small business meetings.

I remember this occasion very well. While I was available serving cocktails to the guests, one of them raised his glass and gave a toast from Shakespeare's play "Julius Caesar." The gentleman's strong voice was loud and clear. He recited, "Tomorrow, and Tomorrow and Tomorrow, Creeps in this petty pace, 'Til the last syllable of recorded time ..blah, blah, blah." And I almost recited the remaining words of the sonnet, "and all our yesterdays have lighted fools the way to dusky death." But luckily, I caught myself and kept silent. Later, in another room, I told Lizzy what I almost did. We had a good laugh.

As her name and service grew, Lizzy picked up another very important engagement with a famous family. This family was the Gordons, who owned the Gordon's Gin distillery. She catered two small dinner parties at their estate in Long Island and was pretty confident that this family would become one of her regular clients.

Elizabeth developed into a very attractive young woman. She was tall, almost 5 feet 8 inches, and weighed between 120-125 pounds. Her skin tone was dark brown and she carefully chose her makeup to accent her very large eyes and round full face. She had a head full of hair, which would have grown down her back had she let it, but Elizabeth did not like long hair and wore it cropped short as soon as she was old enough to make that decision herself.

Elizabeth was a very popular young woman. She had several male friends, but was in no hurry to walk to the altar in marriage with any of them. A city policeman named Smitty became one of her special boyfriends, and she spent a great deal of time with him, but no marriage resulted.

That Terrible Accident

Few people knew that Elizabeth also had a mild heart condition. Indeed, I was not aware of it until she was about 35 years old. It was considered a murmur and she was on medication to keep it in check. This condition pretty well governed and controlled the extent of her activities at this stage of her life.

Elizabeth traveled to Wilson's Mills with Pearlie Vinson, her son, Harold and her sisters Carrie, Aretha, and Carrie's granddaughter to attend the funeral of Mrs. Ada Vinson. Harold did the driving. Following the funeral, this group of individuals was returning to New York with one extra passenger. This nineteen-year-old male asked to ride back with them because he had spent his ticket money and was unable to return by train. Six adults and one eight-month old baby began the journey back to New York. (Note: The City of Wilson is about 35 miles from Smithfield.) However, after leaving Smithfield, traveling North on US Highway 301, and before they reached the City of Wilson, North Carolina, they were involved in a terrible accident.

According to the police report, two sailors traveling south on US Highway 301, under the influence of alcohol, lost control of their car. The vehicle hit an embankment, flew up in the air, and came to rest on top of the Vinsons' car which was traveling north. Everybody was killed in the accident, except the eight-month-old baby girl in the Vinsons' car. It is believed that she was cushioned and sheltered by the woman she sat near or beside. Elizabeth was also killed. She had just turned 40 years old.

When I got the news, I was devastated. Allie was also devastated by our sister's death. She received the news over the telephone and immediately passed out.

Stories from My Early Days

Punch Drunk

Summer was just beginning to peek its flowery head from behind the wintry clouds. It was June: long days, balmy warm evenings and breeze-swept nights.

School was closed for the season and both Elizabeth and I were home for the summer months. Alex had just arrived at our home in Manhattan. He was our first-cousin who lived in Queens, New York and often came into Manhattan to hang out with us.

Alex's exciting news about a wedding reception that afternoon had prompted both Elizabeth and me to finish our house chores early so that we could spend more time dressing ourselves.

The wedding reception would be held at Alex's friend's home up on Seventh Avenue. His name was Alonzo, and he was the nephew of the famous athlete, Jesse Owens. The reception was a special highlight of this Saturday afternoon, and those who were to be in attendance were carefully chosen

Alex was to escort Elizabeth and me. Otherwise, neither of us would be able to attend the reception. It was only a short walk up to where the reception was to be held. We lived at home with our mother and sister Allie on 138th Street between Lenox and 5th Avenues. Alonzo lived on Seventh Avenue, which seemed like around the corner.

The three of us left home early enough to be at the 5 o'clock reception on time. Upon arrival, we found a reception area beautifully decorated and a few young guests milling around. Following the necessary introductions, we soon made ourselves at home.

On one of the tables was a large decorative bowl of pink punch surrounded by matching cups and glasses, napkins, and hors d'ouvres. The bride and groom had not yet arrived, but the guests were enjoying themselves, chatting, eating and drinking.

I was especially drawn to the pink punch. I helped myself and found it very tasty – quite delicious.

Early in the afternoon before the bride and groom arrived, I began to feel woozy. I soon became sick to the stomach and urged Alex to take me home. As we walked home, I became sicker and what was once a short walk, now became one of my longest.

When we arrived home, my mother became alarmed. She quickly undressed me, put me to bed and called the doctor. When the doctor arrived he quickly rushed into my room and began to examine me. Upon completion of his examination, he sat my anxious mother down to give her the news, "your 19 year old daughter, Elsie, is drunk from an excessive amount of wine." Mother was speechless.

Foiled by a Fork

The date of the campus picnic was finally set. We would be going to the Jones Country Picnic Grounds. Buses were lined up to carry those students who had no car. Buses and cars pulled out at 10:00 a.m. that Saturday morning. The cooking crew left early that morning to begin their jobs of preparing the food. All other preparations were also in place. I was not part of the work crew this year, and as a sophomore, my responsibilities were limited. Traditionally, juniors and seniors carried the bulk of responsibilities for these activities. Therefore, my fellow sophomores and I had very little to do.

I was 19 at the time and had no car, so my friends and I boarded one of the buses for the forty-five minute ride to the picnic grounds. About twenty minutes into the trip, about six of my friends and I decided to walk the rest of the way and persuaded the bus driver to let us off during a brief stop for fuel. The driver agreed and let us walk the rest of the way to the picnic grounds.

Unfortunately, the highway divided a short distance from where we decided to walk. When we reached the divide, we had no idea which way to go. Naturally, we took the wrong direction and got lost. After walking quite a distance, we turned around and began our journey back to school.

Meanwhile, the picnic continued. Everyone seemed to be having fun. But concern about my absence and my friends' was heavy upon the minds of both school administrators and students.

By late afternoon, the picnic was over. Everyone packed up his belongings and prepared to return to campus. En route to the campus, my friends and I were spotted walking back toward campus. Our tired, weary band gladly boarded the bus to ride the last twenty minutes back to campus. Everyone was overjoyed to have found us and welcomed us back on the bus.

However, punishment was in order. My friends and I were grounded for one month.

Motoring Mischief

Richard Taylor was my boyfriend. My mother was less than thrilled with the relationship. Primarily because Richard at 44, was 22 years my senior, and divorced, with a young son. The country was in the midst of World War II and Richard was in the Army.

I was a 22 year old college graduate and free and frivolous, as other young college graduates.

This Saturday afternoon, Richard and I planned to attend a cook-out at the home of some of Richard's friends in Stamford, Connecticut. My cousin Mamie Vinson and her boyfriend had also been invited to attend. As was planned, Richard picked me up with Mamie and her friend, and away the four of us went to Stamford for an evening of fun. We were warmly greeted by the family and friends in Stamford, and immediately joined the crowd in frolic, food, fun and drinks.

For some reason, I got the bright idea that I should move Richard's car and park it elsewhere. I had no car of my own, nor did I have a license to drive a car. But Richard often let me drive his car on back streets and country roads. Stamford, Connecticut is a large city, but this did not matter to me at the time. I convinced Mamie to go with me to move the car, and she agreed.

I seated myself in the drivers' seat, did all the correct things, and off we went around the block. Upon our return, I was faced with a parking space that was not only different, but it was also around the corner on an inclined embankment. Instead of asking Richard for help, I decided to try to park the car. I put the car in reverse, pressed the accelerator, and backward I went down the hill until the car came to rest against the barbed-wire fence of a pasture. The car was so securely stuck that a tow truck had to pull it out, several days later. Richard, Mamie, her friend and I had to return to New York by train.

Safe and Sound (Asleep)

Early one Fourth of July morning, my daughters and I were awakened by heavy banging on my front door. Alarmed, I got out of bed, put on my bath robe and dashed to the door. When I finally got the door opened, I was greeted by a New Jersey State Police officer. After showing me his credentials, he began to explain why he was at my home so early in the morning. He had a young man in his custody by the name of Donald Patterson. The officer explained that the young man said he was on his way from his home in New York City to spend the Fourth of July with me and my family. We were told his car was well stocked with food, beverages, fruit, desserts and favors to celebrate Independence Day. However, this young driver was overcome with sleep, and possibly alcohol, while en route to my home. So this Mr. Patterson apparently parked his car on the center island of the New Jersey Turnpike and fell asleep. The trooper and his partner observed his car very early that morning parked in this odd location. They proceeded to find out what the problem was and to remove his car from its position on the Turnpike.

"Do you know him?" asked the trooper. I answered, "Yes, I know him quite well. We were schoolmates at Kittrell College in North Carolina." That seemed to be enough to satisfy the troopers, who then left.

After further discussion, Mr. Patterson locked his car, came inside, made himself comfortable on the living room sofa and went back to sleep. It was 5:00 a.m.

My Intellectual Journey

Smithfield – Johnston County Training School

When I finished the seventh grade at the Short Journey Elementary School for Colored Students, my parents brought me to New York and enrolled me in Jamaica Junior High School in Hillside Heights. Friends, neighbors and I went to school daily. My parents were very pleased, but I was not. Early in November, my parents realized that I was unhappy and missed my grandmother very much. So after a little more than two months, I withdrew from the Jamaica school system and was transferred to the Johnston County Training School in Smithfield, North Carolina.

For the next four years, I remained focused on my school work and performed as an outstanding student. Unlike my elementary school years when I traveled to school by car with teachers each day, now I traveled by bus. Each morning the school bus stopped at the corner of my street in Wilson's Mills. Along with many other students, I took my seat on the bus and traveled the five or six miles to school in Smithfield.

Some of the other students who rode the bus with me were Theresa Vinson, Clarence Sanders, William Smith, Catherine Vinson, Luetta Coley, Emma Lee McCullers, and Quincy Watson. Quincy and Luetta lived in the country so they boarded the bus at a different bus stop.

Being the tomboy that I was, I had learned very well how to protect myself in case there was aggression against me. But I was not the kind of youngster who would begin a fight nor agitate or annoy others so that I would become a nuisance. On the contrary, I tended to be a bit withdrawn, very quiet, and minded my own business. I was very studious and spent a great deal of time reading or doing school work.

At school in Smithfield I was often pestered by the school bully or town bullies. There were times when the bullies would meet the school bus, call me and others by name, point out features they thought were ugly and persist with nasty remarks. Some of the bullies were older and bigger than I, and some were about my age. The school did nothing to stop the bullying, though I never reported incidents to the school authorities either.

School, itself, was fun, exciting and demanding, and I was an industrious student who became a participant in as many school functions as I could. However, because I lived in Wilson's Mills and had no means of transportation to and from the school in the evenings and on weekends, I was limited in the number and types of after-school functions I could select. But I did select and become quite involved in extra curricular activities.

High school debating team. If I couldn't win in matches with bullies, I could win with my ability to present ideas and argue for things I believed in. I joined the debating team and traveled to high schools and colleges to match wits with other students. Moreover, I enjoyed being able to speak in another language also. I could speak French fluently, and went on to obtain a minor in French upon completing my college baccalaureate.

High school chorus. I loved to sing and for three years remained a member of the chorus. The director of the chorus, Joseph Bridges, was efficient and competent. His chorus gave concerts at the colleges throughout the state, at churches, other schools, as well as radio broadcasts. I also traveled with the chorus. My high soprano voice was both supported and needed. Mr. Bridges, however, never complimented me nor acknowledged my presence in the chorus. He was highly impressed by those students with light skin and long flowing hair. I had long hair, but I also had dark skin. Therefore, I was not in his "loop."

I learned a great deal about music, however, during my high school years in the chorus. The music selected by Mr. Bridges for the chorus to sing was of the highest quality. Famous black musicians such as Dr. R. Nathaniel Dett, came as guests to both lecture and demonstrate to the students. The chorus became well known for the spirited rendition of "Listen to the Lambs," and "Go Down Moses." John Watson, whose deep base voice always brought the house down with his rendition of "Ole Man River," was a favorite soloist.

I was the highest honor student throughout my high school year, and graduated valedictorian of my class. Quincy Watson, also of Wilson's Mills, was salutatorian.

Valedictorian of my class. Many years later, I really learned just what my music teacher thought of me. My mother-in-law, Mrs. Isabelle Collins, a noted soloist and pianist, was asked by the minister of a large United Methodist Church in New York City to solo on one particular occasion. The director of music for this church was Mr. Bridges. During a brief conversation with Mr. Bridges, Ms. Isabelle Collins learned that he was from the South and was the chorus director at the Johnston County Training School in Smithfield. She established the connection and was sure that he was my old music teacher. With excitement, she told me about Mr. Bridges and encouraged me to join the church choir there. I became excited and went to choir rehearsal the next Monday night. Bubbling over with excitement, I greeted Mr. Bridges. His response to me was, "I'm sorry, I don't know you. You have the wrong person." I shut my mouth, went home after choir rehearsal, and did not return to that church.

Kittrell College, Kittrell, North Carolina

I received an excellent academic background in elementary education at Short Journey Elementary School for Colored Students. Mrs. Eva J. Cooper, the principal, along with her teachers, enjoyed the reputation of having an outstanding school who prepared her students well. Short Journey's students performed well socially, as well as academically throughout their high school years. Many of these students also became strong community leaders.

While I kept my hopes high, throughout my school years in public education, I felt pursued by that very destructive shadow of segregation and discrimination. No matter how ambitious, intelligent or motivated African American students were, they were denied equal opportunities in every aspect of American life. So when three other students and I from Short Journey Elementary School excelled in the statewide academic test for all students in North Carolina, it caused concern, not congratulations.

Our scores exceeded the highest boundary the state had set for African American students, but also exceeded the highest boundary set for white students. Now, the idea that black students might excel in comparison to white students, at this time, was unthinkable to the white community. This explains why the county school administrator was alarmed. The superintendent of schools, Mr. Marrow, sought to find out what happened. Just why were these colored students' scores higher than those of most of the white students?

Superintendent Marrow visited the Short Journey School. He spoke with the principal, Mrs. Eva J. Cooper, and with those teachers who administered the tests to the seventh graders. He spoke individually with each of the four girls and then spoke to them as a group before leaving the school. The "controversy" continued and the girls met with the superintendent at least two more times. I remember my meetings with Mr. Marrow. He was especially interested in my parents and what kind of work they did.

Students from Short Journey School continued to excel on the statewide academic tests. However, when a young African American male made a perfect score on the geography segment of the test and excelled in all other aspects of the statewide test, he was not acknowledged either. Statewide and national awards given to students in recognition of their academic achievements were not available to non-white students, but went to white students, only. Ultimately, our superior achievement was simply ignored. My friends and I received no awards. However, I entered high school well prepared academically and graduated four years later, in 1940, as valedictorian of my class.

I entered Kittrell College as a freshman in 1940 and found myself among a different type of student body, one that was much different from the high school group that I had just left.

A few of Kittrell's students were older than my eighteen-years. However, some were adults, some were married, and some were ministers.

And some even had a limited or poor academic foundation and needed tutoring so they could keep up with the professors' requirements. However, most students were high school graduates, like myself, who were simply attending college.

I had no trouble keeping up and meeting all the academic requirements of all my professors. I soon developed the reputation of being extremely smart, and my professors began to challenge me by giving extra assignments to complete. This was especially true of my math Professor, Mr. Luna I. Mishoe, my history Professor Dr. Walton, and my French Professor, Dr. D'Arce`.

I was required to work and help put myself through school. During my freshman year, I worked in the dining hall as a "busboy" for breakfast. My job was to help set the tables, and serve food during the first semester. I was also assigned to a tutoring position. Therefore, my job in the kitchen was eventually discontinued.

For the second semester, I was assigned to the Housekeeping Department with the responsibility of making up beds and straightening up a number of rooms in the girls' dormitories. I was also assigned to a tutoring responsibility.

My mother was having a very difficult time meeting her financial responsibilities in New York. To keep me at Kittrell became a struggle for mother. Dad had separated himself completely from the family. We children had no contact with him after he moved out. We saw him now and then and exchanged greetings, but he did not visit with us at all.

Finally, I was called into a very important meeting with the college President Dr. Dent, and the college academic dean, Dr. Scott. There was a dilemma and it had to be discussed. I was to be dismissed from the college due to a lack of funds. I was told that though I was an asset to the college, and they really did not want to dismiss me, but my financial debt needed attention now. The college administration decided to keep me the rest of the school year if I would agree to be responsible for the total unpaid college debt. At the end of the school year, they decided to submit the total bill to me, which included all monies owed for the two years I had spent at Kittrell. The bill also stipulated the amount of money I was required to pay each month until the bill was paid. I was therefore allowed to complete my second year at Kittrell.

For the second year, my work detail was changed. I became a full-time tutor in three major academic subjects (Math, French and U.S. History) with longer hours. I took these college responsibilities in stride. You might think all this might have discouraged me. It didn't. I knew I would get a college degree eventually – and my family expected nothing less of me and other family members.

Sally Baldwin became one of my closest friends. She was also my mentor and functioned as a positive catalyst for all of the younger girls. Sally, who was almost seven years my senior, got married during our freshman year at Kittrell. Her husband was Arthur Howard, a few years older than Sally, but not a student at Kittrell.

Sally organized a quartet of four girls, and I was the soprano singer. Sally sang tenor, Idell sang alto, and Edna sang bass. Miss Lucas, the college music professor, became interested in the musical group, gave her encouragement, and played for us as often as she could. As the musical group or BEA's (our group name) grew in popularity and expertise, we were invited to sing at civic and church functions. During one occasion, we brought embarrassment upon ourselves. At the General Conference Meeting in Baltimore, Maryland, the Presiding Bishop Davis invited individuals and organizations from Kittrell to attend. The BEA's were among those invited to participate on Sunday afternoon, the highlight and last day of the General Conference.

Transportation to Baltimore to attend the conference was arranged by the college for BEA's. All went well. Finally, the evening of the performance arrived. We found ourselves before a huge audience performing at our very best. For some reason, Sally stopped singing, and appeared to be holding back laughter. I did not see Sally, but Edna did, and she also stopped singing and became filled with laughter. Meanwhile, we continued to sing unaware of the fact that only two of us were singing. When it became apparent that there was a problem with the group, I leaned forward to look at Sally and determine what was wrong. When I looked at Sally's face and discovered that it was broken up in laughter, laughter also overwhelmed me and then the entire quartet became hysterical with laughter. Miss Lucas, the pianist and music instructor, stopped playing, ordered us to sit down and offered an apology. The Bishop also spoke to us girls as well and offered an apology to the congregation. After the BEA's got ourselves together, we appeared again on the program, and were a great success.

Sally had another significant influence upon me, and that was to enhance my love of poetry. Sally was very good at reciting poetry and was especially good at acting out some of Paul Laurence Dunbar's monologues. Her favorite ones were, "When Malindy Sings," and "A Negro Love Song." I learned this style of poetic expression from her. In addition to those poems, I added to my repertoire Dunbar's "In the Morning," and became quite good at acting out poetry in a monologue.

Delaware State College (now Delaware State University)

In the fall of 1943, I matriculated at Delaware State College. With careful and skillful planning of my funds, supplemented with regular help from my mother, I was able to meet my entire financial responsibility to Kittrell College. Therefore, my college records were transferred to Delaware State College in good standing. Because of my excellent grades and academic standing, I was admitted to Delaware State College as an advanced junior in September, the fall of 1943.

I matriculated at Delaware State College because of Miss Davis. Miss Davis, daughter of the Bishop of the AME Conference, was Dean of Women at Kittrell during my freshman year. But Miss Davis, who soon after became Dean of Women at Delaware State, felt that Kittrell did not challenge me academically, socially nor educationally. She wrote and told my mother that I should attend a more challenging college and suggested Delaware State College.

When I arrived at Delaware State, there was a new Dean of Women. Miss Davis had gotten married and moved with her husband to the State of Maryland. She became Dean of Women at Morgan State College in Baltimore, Maryland.

I had no trouble readjusting to college life. Immediately, I settled in and assumed my academic responsibilities. I remained on the Dean's List over the next two years, making A's and some B's in all of my subjects. I was considered by everyone as a student in the high, or even highest, honor category.

I also immediately became involved in student activities and affairs. The debating skills I developed in high school paid off and I soon became the college's major representative on the debating team and traveled to both Philadelphia and New York City to participate in the major debating tournaments.

Small in Stature, But ...

At 90-95 pounds and standing about 5'1", I was a small individual, almost twenty years old. But my size did not stop me from being a star athlete. I was counted among the fastest and best guards on the girl's basketball team. Since French was one of my three minors – English and Math were the other two – I spoke French fluently and became President of the French club. My rich experiences in the high school glee club prepared me for the dominant role music would play in my life, subsequently. I was in the college choir and would become a major soloist for the college. The college's music director, Mrs. Genevieve Wisner, recognized my musical abilities and began to train my voice for recitals and concerts. I was called to represent the college instead of the choir on some occasions.

I also enjoyed journalism. As a junior, I was Assistant Editor of the college newspaper – "The Hornet," and became Editor-in-Chief in my senior year. While I was competent and capable, I was not an out-going social leader. I tended to be quiet and a bit shy. Flirting with young men was not anything I bothered to do.

World War II had taken most of the young men off the college campuses and sent them overseas. The few young men who were left were either married, in great demand by the girls, or were servicemen who were attending college part-time. I was also considered a New Yorker, which caused special interest among my colleagues. My clothing and some mannerisms reflected a New York lifestyle. My mother came down from New York to visit me whenever it was appropriate. I went home to New York, probably, once a month. My Uncle Lee and Aunt Anna provided a written excuse to the college for me to spend some weekends with them in Philadelphia when the Penn Relays or other activities occurred.

Who's Who Among Seniors was determined by a vote of the student body each year. I was voted the "Senior Most Likely to Succeed" among students in my graduating class.

However, the old problem of color racism among black Americans (the favoring of those with lighter complexions) became brutally evident at Delaware State College in my senior year. Academic excellence over the past two to three years had already determined which students in the senior class had achieved highest honors, high honors, and honors. It was a generally accepted fact that I - Elsie McIntosh – would either be the student with the highest honor or certainly high honors. A shock wave passed through the student body, especially the senior class, when the Dean's List was posted and my name was *not* among the top honors group. Instead, I was listed among the students with B or better averages who also graduated with honors.

... In a Category of My Own

Discontent and statements of "unfair" moved among the student body, especially the senior class until it reached the office of the President, Dr. Howard Decca Gregg. Shortly thereafter, the list was withdrawn and revised. On the revised list a third category had been created, and my name appeared in this category. This category stated High Honors with Outstanding Contributions to Academics and Campus Life. This category was satisfactory to me and it also calmed tempers among the graduating class.

The college choir leader, under the direction of Mrs. Wisner, rendered some outstanding music for the commencement exercises. Two of the songs they sang were as follows, "Somebody's Knocking at Your Door," and "O Lord Most Holy." I was the soloist for both selections. When I came across the stage to receive my degree, Dr. Gregg, College President, paused to talk about me at length. It seemed longer than he had spoken about any of the other students in my class. And, of course, he made remarks about each student as he shook his/her hand.

In the audience was an individual from the Westminster Choir College, Princeton, New Jersey, who came up to me shortly after the commencement exercises. This individual offered me a Fellowship to get a Master's degree in Music (Voice) at Westminsters' Choir College. I was told that my voice had great potential and with the proper training I could possibly, eventually become famous.

I was interested, for I truly loved music, and enjoyed singing very much. But I could not afford to take advantage of this opportunity; my mother needed my financial help. Although my mother was in her late forties, I saw signs of wear and tear on her body, and knew she needed help. I decided to go to work. I accepted a job teaching social studies at Booker T. Washington Junior High School in Dover, Delaware at age 22.

Teachers College, Columbia University – New York City, NY

Following several conversations with my mother, I decided to enter graduate school and get a Master's degree. Although Teachers College, Columbia University was so much closer to home than New York University (NYU), I chose NYU because my friends, Rita Bunyan, Richard White and Mary Seaman were students there.

It was explained to me by my advisor at NYU that I had to complete 15 credits in certain required courses before I could be admitted to graduate school. I completed the 15 credits as required over a couple of summers, but was denied admission. They explained to me that I did not have the capacity to do graduate work. Therefore, my request for admission was denied.

That same summer, I went right over to Columbia University, met with an advisor and enrolled. I was also told that I would have to complete 15 credits in certain required subjects before I could be admitted to graduate school. Over the next two summers, I completed the required 15 credits. My advisor explained that I had the capacity to do rigorous graduate work, and was therefore admitted in good standing to Teachers College, Columbia University.

I began my graduate program in the summer of 1947 and continued to carry a full load for five consecutive summers, finishing in the summer of 1951. The program was rigorous; the responsibilities demanding; and the cost high. But I met the challenge. My field of study was "The Teaching of US History and the Social Studies in Secondary Schools." I also knew that I had to pass a comprehensive examination before completing all requirements leading to a master's degree. I was also told that the examination would be quite difficult, but that candidates/ students are given three opportunities to take it and succeed.

I had never been a good test-taker, I always tended to freeze up and fall apart. And I was afraid I would do so on the comprehensive exam at Columbia.

The Comprehensive Exams were an all-day encounter at the University. Tests were given on Saturdays. I took the comprehensive the fourth summer of summer school and was relieved but drained when I came home.

A few days later, I met with my advisor to discuss the test results. The test was divided into two major parts: 1) an essay of ten comprehensive questions to be fully discussed, and 2) 250 short answer questions a candidate would need four to five hours to complete. My test results were less than satisfactory. I answered correctly – all of the 250 questions and most of the essay questions, but the advisor explained that I had not give an extensive enough discussion in answering half of the essay questions. For that reason, I was required to take the essay portion of the exam again.

In preparation to take the essay portion of the Comprehensive Examination, the fifth summer, I met frequently with my advisor. He assured me that I would pass this time.

I allowed fear to overwhelm me during the week of preparation. The Thursday prior to the Saturday of the exam, I became ill with chills and an upset stomach severe enough for my family doctor to send me to Sydenham Hospital for a physical examination. Dr. Wiley Martin and other medical team members examined me thoroughly and found no physical problems. I remained at the hospital Thursday night and most of Friday. My family members brought to my hospital room my books, notes, pencils and notepads. I studied, preparing for the test I was to take in a few days. I tried to calm down, was reassured that I was not physically ill, and I was encouraged to take the test on Saturday. I was released from the hospital Friday and went to Columbia University on Saturday morning to take the short essay portion of my comprehensive exam in a relaxed frame of mind. My advisor informed me later that I had passed the short essay portion of the comprehensive exam with flying colors.

During the summer sessions when I was a student at Columbia University, I was also employed as a full-time social studies teacher at the Booker T. Washington Junior High School in Dover, Delaware. When school closed in May, I went home to New York, where I stayed until school opened in September each year. Because I was home and lived quite near Columbia University, I was able to spend a great deal of time daily at the University participating in a variety of activities. But, of course, naturally, my very special interest was in the Summer Session Chorus at Teachers College. I took the elective, all-college chorus, under the direction of Dr. Harry R. Wilson, and remained in the chorus for the next seven summers. During this time, I was selected by Dr. Wilson as a member of the traveling chorus of 44 voices who performed at special events conducted by the University. Gen. Dwight D. Eisenhower was President of Columbia University at this time, and I recall a time when he was a guest speaker at Montclair State College in New Jersey. The chorus of 44 voices accompanied him and others to this affair and I was with the chorus of 44 voices. One of the requirements to participate in this group was to participate in voice lessons at the University about three times per week. Every summer in July and August, the summer session chorus of 200 voices gave concerts – one at the People's Church, Columbia University, and the second was an orchestral and choral concert held in the McMillan Theatre at the University.

I also held down a summer job to provide extra money to meet my needs. One of my jobs, which I considered most rewarding, was teaching Vacation Bible School at the Abyssinian Baptist Church in Harlem. The church was located up the street only one block from my home on 138th street between 7th and Lenox Avenues. Many of my students lived in the neighborhood. My general boss was Congressman, The Rev. Adam Clayton Powell, Jr. Because of his responsibilities in Washington, D.C., Congressman Powell was unable to meet weekly with his summer staff, but he did arrange to spend quality time with us when necessary. For three consecutive summers, beginning in 1953, I was one of the Vacation Bible School teachers at Abyssinian Baptist Church.

My mother had passed away in 1950, before I had completed a master's degree program at Columbia University. During one of my visits to my grandmother's home in Wilson's Mills, North Carolina, I came up with the fine idea of persuading my grandmother to attend the ceremonies at the University when I graduated. I had already established the pattern of going to Wilson's Mills during my Christmas break from school, and bringing my grandmother back to New York to spend the winter and spring with me and Allie. During the spring break in May, I would take my grandmother back to Wilson's Mills. Commencement ceremonies at Columbia would be held June 2nd and I wanted my grandmother, who had always been a major part of my life, to attend. To my delight, she agreed.

I carefully planned my strategy so that my grandmother would be safe, and be able to see "her Elsie." There would be thousands of people in attendance outside, utilizing most areas. My grandmother and I left home early, arrived at the campus early enough to select a particular seat in a particular area. I gave my grandmother instructions not to move from her seat under any circumstances, and she didn't. It was a fascinating experience for her as she watched her granddaughter march in a sea of long robes of many colors. Twelve thousand students graduated that day. My grandmother also saw General Eisenhower in his role of University President. The year was 1952 and I was proud as could be to graduate from what is considered by many to be the premier teachers college in the nation.

Becoming a Professor

By the late 1960s I had over a decade of teaching experience under my belt. As a teacher, seeking a doctorate was not a priority on my list. As a matter of fact, I really had no desire to seek one. Most of the members of my old "gang" of professional colleagues from Columbia had master's degrees. A couple had bachelor's degrees; my brother-in-law was a high school graduate, and two "gang" members had a doctorate.

Most of us, however, were involved in some extensive academic studies that were related to our professions. I had completed extensive professional work at colleges and universities near Trenton. My certificate in the "Teaching of Urban Studies" was earned at Rutgers University in New Brunswick, New Jersey. I also completed a program called "Teacher Participation in Curriculum Design" at Princeton University and received a certificate for that program. My master's degree from Teachers College at Columbia University, the workshops required by the school districts, plus additional academic work, prepared me well to meet any academic challenges that came my way.

In 1971, colleagues suggested I apply for a teaching position at Trenton State College. I became very enthusiastic about the idea. But one of the first things I learned was that to remain an instructor I had to obtain a doctoral degree.

Among my many friends urging me to accept this position was my friend and colleague, Dr. Joe M. Smith. Joe was a recent graduate of Union Institute and had maintained administrative contacts with that university. He would make sure I got an application to the University and urged me to apply for admission.

In private conferences with Dr. Bernard Schwartz, my department chair, and Dr. Clayton Brower, President of the College, I accepted their invitation to join the faculty at Trenton State College (now, The College of New Jersey). I also informed each that I would matriculate at a university immediately and begin work toward a doctorate.

The college would guarantee me a tenured position as Assistant Professor for a period of four years as long as I was matriculated in pursuit of my doctorate. However, if the four-year period ended prior to the completion of the doctoral program, tenure would automatically be granted because I was in a doctoral program.

During discussion at Trenton State College regarding my acceptance of the professorial position and the responsibilities that accompanied it, I was also informed by my department chair, Dr. Bernard Schwartz, that I had to become certified as a supervisor in order to oversee the education of students in any state. This meant that I was charged with two very important tasks that had to be accomplished within the next four to five years; 1) become a certified supervisor; and 2) earn a doctorate.

After making a very important telephone call to the State Department of Education, I learned that the required courses in administration and supervision were being offered at Rider University (at the time Rider College). After speaking with an advisor, I learned that since I already had a master's degree, I would be required to earn an additional 12-15 credits in curriculum construction/revision, administrative styles and philosophy and staff development and supervision. After two years of intensive study, I earned my certificate and could function in every state with which the State of New Jersey has reciprocity, almost all 50.

Getting a Doctorate

The application for admission to the doctoral program at Union finally came. It was long and complicated, as most university applications are. I was able to answer most of the questions with ease, but there were two questions that presented a challenge and required personal discipline and personal research to answer with satisfaction. These questions were as follows: "Who are you?" "Show or explain how and why your doctoral research would contribute to the betterment of humankind." I was quite sure I could answer these two questions on a few pages and be done. Not so! A synthesis was required in which one's philosophy, cultural experiences and lifestyle, plus the accumulation of academic background, would have to be integrated. I needed help. After conferences with Dr. Smith, Dr. Schwartz, and Dr. Bill Parker, I was finally able to figure out how to explain who I am.

With a bit more clarity, my advisory group was able to help me select a research topic that would be connected to who I am, and would also be of benefit to others. My research topic was "Dynamics of Institutional Change: A Study of the Process to Develop Alternative Programs in Teacher Education in a Multipurpose College." This research kept me intensely and extensively busy. I was in attendance at colloquia which lasted from two-weeks to six-weeks at New York University, New York, New York, and St. Petersburg College in St. Petersburg, Florida; in conferences with educational historians from Princeton and Dr. Sam Proctor from Rutgers, the State University, all under the intense guidance and demands of my doctoral committee. Dr. Carruthers, Professor, University of Chicago, was my core faculty member and the administrator of the committee. Dr. Bernard Schwartz, my department chair, was the on-task commander and an expert in higher education. He made sure that I fully addressed all aspects of my topic.

I ran into a serious challenge when Dr. William Parker brought up a concern that aroused the curiosity of the entire committee. His concern was the presence of so few African-American students seeking college degrees from state colleges in the State of New Jersey. This new question sent me in search of many early 20th century graduates/

attendees as I could find – white and non-white. I found a few examples, but perhaps the most interesting and well informed individual helpful to my inquiry was Dr. James J. Forcina, once Acting President of Trenton State College. He talked to me both on and off the record, and I found him to be highly informative.

Following four years of intensive study, research and writing, I completed all doctoral requirements of the university and the degree was conferred upon me in 1977. My dissertation was printed by the Princeton University Press and distributed to the appropriate individuals at the conferring ceremony.

Being Sorted: Social Class and Complexion

Social Class in Dover

When I came to the Booker T. Washington Junior High School in Dover to begin my teaching career, I also stepped into a well-defined class system that existed among the African American society. I was 22 years old and both academically and socially prepared to meet society's challenges. According to Dover's class system, I was a pretty good candidate for the upper-middle class stratum of African Americans.

I acquired the name of "Mac" (short for McIntosh) during my college days at Delaware State and I soon became known as "Mac" to everyone.

I had just graduated from Delaware State College in May. It was now October 1945, and I had just arrived in Dover to take over my first teaching job. I was given this job as a last resort and that was because the last six teachers of this particular class had either been run out of the class of eighth graders or had simply left the class for other reasons. Whatever the case, these children had no teacher this late in the school year, and I was offered the position. As a matter of fact, it was my mother who answered the phone that Wednesday evening when Mr. Marcellus Blackburn, Principal of the school, called. He was looking for a Social Studies/English teacher for his school, and wanted to know whether or not Miss Elsie E. McIntosh was available. After finding out just what the phone call was all about, my mother said yes and began to jump for joy. She also promised Mr. Blackburn that I would be in Dover over the weekend and ready to take over the position at the school on Monday morning.

My mother then called the Bedfords, told them the good news about the job offer at Booker T. Washington Junior High School, and then asked them if I could live with them during the school year.

Mother felt comfortable talking to Mildred and Joe Bedford. She had met them at Delaware State College while I was a student there. My roommate, during my junior year, was Lydia Perkins, a young lady from Seaford, Delaware. Since this was the same town that Mildred Bedford was from, Lydia and Mildred knew each other very well. During my mother's visits to the college on Parents Day and other special occasions, she had an opportunity to become acquainted with several parents and others, including the Belford's.

Mildred and Joe Bedford promised my mom they would find a home for me, and they did. My mother and I came down from New York on Friday evening. We spent the weekend with the Bedfords while I moved into my new home with Mrs. Lillian Sockum and got ready for school on Monday morning. Mrs. Sockum was the first grade teacher at Booker T. and Mildred Bedford was the fourth grade teacher. Mr. Bedford was the Principal of Harrington Elementary School. I was well placed. Families whose objectives were congruent to those of my own family's surrounded me.

I was not class conscious for I did not know what that meant. But I had grown up in a family of educators, as well as individuals with well defined, achievable goals, such as midwives, teachers, nurses, ministers, dieticians, lawyers and some were doctors. Therefore, I had, sort of, inherited upper middle class values.

I was not familiar with the quaint little town of Dover (population about 20,000) that was the home of Delaware State College. I did not know the townspeople other than those who taught at the college: Mrs. G. Wisner, the choir director; Mrs. B. Henry, the college organist and professor of music; Mrs. Lillian Sockum, with whom I lived; Mr. Blackburn, the school principal; and the Bedfords. However, I was quickly embraced by the educators and other professionals, and was considered, it seems, a member of the privileged middle-class.

A few months after I became a member of the faculty at Booker T. Washington School, I received a letter from Principal Blackburn. The letter read as follows: "If you do not join Whatcoat Methodist Church, where I belong, I will not recommend your return to Booker T. Washington School to teach next year."

I had not joined any church, nor any choir since arriving in Dover because I was new to the community. At college, I attended the nondenominational assembly services, which were held each Sunday morning under the direction of the college chaplain. However, I was African Methodist Episcopal (AME) by family tradition and my Uncle Rev. Purl Richardson was quite a strong voice in that denomination, as well. That might be one reason why Rev. Matthews, minister of the AME church in Dover, invited me to attend services there some time. He reminded me that I was an old AME like himself.

But I joined Whatcoat; mainly because of the warning letter I received from my school principal. I also joined the choir, became the principal soloist, and joined the Young Adult Fellowship, as well.

Professor Genevieve Wisner, music professor at the Delaware State College, was very civic-minded, and held membership in several national organizations. One was the National Organization of Negro Women, which was founded by Mrs. Mary McLeod Bethune. When the National Conference met in Washington, DC, Professor Wisner took me to the conference with her. We spent the weekend in Washington, and I had the opportunity to meet many prominent women, one of which was Mrs. Bethune. Professor Wisner also gave me piano lessons, once or twice per week at her home, and encouraged me to practice as often as possible at her home. Mrs. Wisner was from Denver, Colorado.

Professor Wisner was the mother of four sons. Since the death of her husband, she was left with the responsibility of raising her sons and making sure they were properly educated. Three of her sons were college graduates and two of these sons were married. They all lived in nearby states. The youngest son was attending Delaware State, and lived at home. Professor Wisner had no daughters and often told me that she felt like I was her own daughter.

Professor Wisner was also a member of the Alpha Kappa Alpha Sorority. There were no Greek organizations for women in Dover. My previous involvement in the affairs of Greek-life was limited; but Mrs.

Wisner involved me as much as possible. In 1949, Epsilon Iota Omega Chapter of Alpha Kappa Alpha Sorority was formed. I was one of the charter members.

After we became close, this faculty member so dear to me accepted the position as Professor of Music at Morgan State College in Baltimore, Maryland and left Delaware State College. Her move saddened me very much.

Mrs. Beatrice Henry was also a Professor of Music at Delaware State College, and was also the organist of Whatcoat Methodist Church. She was a quiet, dignified woman from Washington, D.C., and had completed both her undergraduate and master's program at Howard University. She had also done further study in music and the organ at Temple University in Philadelphia, Pennsylvania. She was married to Dr. Charles Henry, a prominent African American Dentist in Dover. Dr. Charles Henry was the nephew of Dr. William Henry of Dover. Dr. William Henry was a medical doctor, and like Mrs. Beatrice Henry, both he and Dr. Charles were graduates of Howard University.

Mrs. Henry was also interested in cultivating my voice. She, just as Mrs. Wisner had done, selected operatic music and early church music for me to study and learn; music by Bach, Mozart, Verdi, Handel and so on, which would strengthen my voice and prepare me for concerts. Weekly, I went to Mrs. Henry's home and rehearsed. I learned new music and/or rehearsed for recitals. Frequently, Mrs. Henry and I appeared in a concert/recital. On one occasion, Mrs. Marie Frazier, Mrs. Henry and I were featured in concert. It was presented in this way: after the audience was seated and each section of the concert completed, I would come on stage, bow to the audience, proceed to the organ, adjust the stops and arrange the music on the organ in the order it was to be played, in preparation for Mrs. Henry. At least once a month, usually, the first Sunday, I was featured in a solo at church. Songs among my repertoire were, Molotte's "The Lord's Prayer," Schubert's "Ave Maria," "O'Divine Redeemer," from "Elijah," Alleluia, several solos from Handel's "The Messiah," and so on. I was pressed into membership in the "Bridge Club." Dr. and Mrs. Charles Henry had no children, so I became a kind of daughter for Mrs. Henry. We became very close and remained friends long after I left the State of Delaware.

When Mrs. Henry died suddenly of a heart attack in the mid 1980's, I traveled to Dover to attend her funeral. It was held in the Chapel of Delaware State College.

The Shock: "Mac" is Black

One of the white professors at Delaware State College became infatuated with me and was determined to make me his girlfriend. This young man, whose name was Arnold (pseudonym), was Jewish and an only child of a wealthy business family in North Jersey. The family business was founded by his grandfather and was now in the hands of his father and uncle. But subsequently, Arnold would be expected to manage it. Now, at age 27, he was already being groomed for this responsibility.

Arnold also had a second career in music and had completed his master's program at Barnard College, Columbia University in Orchestral Music.

Arnold was quite handsome with dark hair, an olive complexion and a sporty mustache. But his attention to me was a bit frightening, for in the 1950's in the State of Delaware, the separation of the races was not just expected but enforced. Although the college was integrated with some white students and faculty, nothing else was.

I finally became attracted to Arnold when he continued to pursue me, so I sought advice from Mrs. Henry as how to respond to his overtures. Mrs. Henry advised me to allow him to visit and also accompany him at affairs on the college campus, but do not associate with him in town, or other public places which might suggest integration. I explained this arrangement to Arnold and why it had to be this way. It was because we were in Delaware and not in New York, nor New Jersey. He was agreeable.

Arnold called me "Mac" – short for McIntosh – or "My Little Indian Squaw" (based on one elaborate costume he put together for me for a costume ball we attended). One of his fellow Jewish professors at the college discovered that the name Mac and "My Little Indian Squaw" referred to an African American girl, and called Arnold's parents. He told them that their son was heavily involved with this person, and thought they should know.

Arnold's mother was more than a bit upset; she was almost hysterical and threatened to take her life if he did not cut off the relationship. By that time, he and I had become very good friends. We had gone to New York at the same time on several occasions, where we could attend plays and concerts downtown together without causing a major stir. Arnold was a member of an orchestral organization, which provided the music for plays, operas, shows, etc., off-Broadway. Whenever his group played, he asked that I accompany him. I did as often as I could. His parents were quite familiar with the name "Mac," but they had no idea that Mac was "black," and the realization seemed to all but kill Arnold's mother. We ended our relationship "cold turkey." He then resigned from his position at the college and went home. I understand he eventually got a MBA from Barnard College at Columbia University.

A Singing Career is Short-Circuited

Howard Stevenson, a young mortician, opened up his business in Dover and became quite successful. On the occasions when he held funerals in his chapel, he would ask me to be in charge of the congregational singing. Howard would make the statement during the funeral that Miss McIntosh will now lead the congregation in the singing of the next hymn. For this participation, he would give me five or ten dollars.

Mr. Fred Forte, President of the New York Chapter of the Johnston County Training School Alumni Association, while in conversation with me, learned that I was a concert artist, and would be happy to do a concert for the Alumni Association as a fundraiser. Mr. Forte was quite excited about the idea, but since he was in no position to judge quality or the possible success of such a project, he told me that he would contact Mr. Bridges about the matter and get back to me regarding next steps.

Mr. Bridges, an African American, was the director of the high school chorus at Johnston County Training School when I was a student there. I was in the chorus from grades nine through eleven, when I graduated.

Mr. Bridges told Mr. Forte and the delegation that went to talk with him about sponsoring me in concert in Smithfield, that I "could not sing at all." He admitted I was in the high school chorus, but said I was not effective and that he put up with me because I was drowned out by the other voices. "Do not sponsor her," was his recommendation. And so, they did not.

I had the painful responsibility of telling Mrs. Henry who would accompany me and serve as my manager and accompanist that the project was off because my former high school chorus director said that I had no talent. Mrs. Henry, was more than disappointed, for she had planned an elaborate concert for us and in addition she had planned to make a substantial donation to the Alumni Association. I thought of writing a rather strong letter to President Forte and Mr. Bridges, but later decided against it.

I believe that Mr. Bridges' dislike for me goes back to my dark skin tone. I remember the clear distinction he made in his treatment of the light skinned chorus members, and the dark skinned chorus members in high school, favoring those with a lighter complexion.

A few years later, Mr. Forte learned I was featured in a successful music program at Tindly Temple Methodist Church in Philadelphia. He was embarrassed and quite ashamed of himself for not seeking other sources of information about my musical ability and he apologized for his behavior every time he saw me.

Mixing It Up: A Segregated USO is Integrated

However, the Dover Air Force Base did steadily grow. Soon it would be the largest Military Air Transport Service (MATS) base of the United States Armed Forces. But, it had one big problem or flaw, if you will. Because of the discriminatory and segregation laws enforced by the State of Delaware, African American airmen were not allowed to be entertained at the USO in town. Only the White airmen were allowed to enter the building and be entertained. This had to be corrected, and so steps were taken to do so.

One afternoon, Lola Tue, a young, black teacher and community worker in Dover, called me. She explained that she was asked to form a select committee of eight girls to work on a very special project. The project was to integrate the USO and thus make its services available to all U.S. airmen or servicemen, regardless of race, culture or ethnicity. She invited me to be one of the selected girls. I accepted.

This committee of eight girls – four black and four white – was very effective. We were involved in planned association with selected airmen for the experiment. All of them learned the dances that were peculiar to both the white race and the black race. We played different games that each race was familiar with; we entered into conversations about selected topics that were familiar to the different racial groups. We learned how to begin a conversation with white and black airmen and were warned against key words or topics that could lead to trouble. I enjoyed my work with the airmen and met a lot of very interesting men. The requirement of the Integration Committee took the girls on base and into the Commissioned, as well as the Non-Commissioned officers' clubs. Delaware's segregation laws, which affected the men/women at the Dover MATS base and the USO, were eventually changed or removed.

Getting Out the Vote

At the polls, vote Republican was the prevailing disposition in Dover. Around election time, everyone was busy "getting out the vote," and Mrs. Weston and her husband were no exception. My first experience with actually going to the polls to vote was done in Dover. I was excited and voted my conscience. Also, my first experience with working for a political party was in Dover. Mr. and Mrs. Weston had a big dinner in the large dining room of their home around each election time. Many people came to eat, both white and black. Mrs. Weston, or someone working for the political party, recruited the young teachers to work as waiters. I was always one of those chosen to work. I enjoyed the exposure to Delaware's politicians, both white and black. I was able to place faces and people with positions and connections, and I enjoyed the ability to make associations. I earned $5-10 for my services.

A Teaching Career Begins

I had a full and active social life after I began to teach school at Booker T. Washington Junior High School in Dover. My male friends were upwardly mobile and contributed to my personal goals and objectives. These men were colleagues, not lovers, and I enjoyed going out with them, dining with them, and often, just chatting with them. The core of friends included the following gentlemen:

Captain James "Jimmy" Cooper, Dover Air Force Base;
Captain William Matthews, Dover Air Force Base;
Master Sergeant Nathan Woody, Dover Air Force Base;
Major M. Armstrong, Classified Activities, Dover Air Force Base;
Paul Rosenfeld, Instructor, Delaware State College;
Howard Stevenson, Owner of Howard W. Stevenson Funeral Home;
Napoleon Pinckney, medical student, Albany, New York;
Romeo Cherot (Rhodes Scholar), Voice of America, Radio Free Europe;
Granville Hay; Administrator, Abyssian Baptist Church, New York City;
Conrad Clarke, feature writer and reporter, Amsterdam News, New York City; and
Fagen Gray, Secret Service, United States Government.

I also had a busy life furthering my education during these fifteen years in Dover, Delaware. It was during that time that I matriculated as a full-time student at Teachers College, Columbia University to seek my master's degree. For the next five years, I attended six weeks of summer school, beginning in June right after regular school closed, and ending the second week in August. In 1952, I graduated from Columbia University, perhaps the most revered teachers college in the nation, with a master's degree in the Teaching of the Social Studies.

Single, Married, Then Single Again

Single in Dover

A single woman, I was proud of my accomplishments both at home in New York and in Dover, where I was teaching. It was evident I was thought of as an excellent teacher, for it seemed that everyone in the town of Dover knew me and prized me for being tough, but fair and open-minded.

While some admired me for a lively mind, others admired my physique. For example, Smitty, a friend of the family, had often referred to my body as perfectly shaped. A member of New York City police force, Smitty was also a small businessman. His family owned a picture gallery and studio on 125th Street in Harlem, New York. Smitty was one of its major part-time photographers. Clearly, he had some expertise in this field. Over a period of a few years, Smitty frequently sought to take a full-length picture of me in the nude to put on display in the family's studio. Modest as I am about my body, he was never able to convince me to pose for such photos.

I was also a style-setter. My clothes were always of the latest fashion and quality, and I endeavored to wear them well. Many positive comments were made about the way I looked in my clothes, as well as how I carried myself.

I was also very much involved in school, church, and community affairs and activities. I was a charter member of the Epsilon Iota Omega

Chapter of the Alpha Kappa Alpha Sorority; assigned as a participant in the Integration Experience of the Dover Air Force Base USO; church soloist and member of the Young Adults Fellowship Group of Whatcoat United Methodist Church; and a concert artist and member of the Dover Bridge Club.

During the fifteen years that I taught school in Dover, I lived in three different homes. These homes served as parenting homes for me, where I was treated as a member of the family, chastised when necessary, and always given sound advice just as parents would do. I was cooperative and respectful, and regarded these families as my own.

The first home that I lived in was that of Mrs. Lillian R. Sockum, first grade teacher at Booker T. Washington Junior High School, where I also taught. Mrs. Sockum was asked by the Bedfords to keep me just one year, and I would be able to stay with them the next year and thereafter. The Bedfords' baby son, Joe Jr. (age two), would stay with Mildred's mother and father in Seaford, Delaware when he became three years old. And Mildred Bedford would also return to her teaching position at Booker T. Washington school. So for that reason, I stayed with Mrs. Sockum one year.

The next year I moved in with the Bedfords and stayed nine years. The Bedfords' second son, Nicholas, was born in 1948. As the boys grew up, it became apparent that the family needed more space for comfort. I was asked to give up my room. I did so, and moved into the home of Courtney and William (Buddy) Stevenson. Here I lived for the next five years. Toward the end of that period, I met and married Douglas Collins and moved to Brooklyn, New York. The year was 1960.

Meeting Douglas

The Methodist Conference of Southern Jersey, Delaware and Maryland sent Rev. Douglas M. Collins, Sr. to Whatcoat Methodist Church in Dover, as pastor. He and his wife, Isabelle C. Collins, moved into the parsonage on Queens Street. Their oldest son, Douglas, frequently came to visit with his parents in Dover. Isabelle's cousin, Reilly Crews, also frequented the church as a visitor. It soon became clear that both of these men were seeking my attention.

I was very popular among the young men of the town, especially commissioned and non-commissioned officers of the Dover Air Force

Base. My most recent male friend was Commissioned officer Murriell Armstrong, who was attached to some sort of high secrecy operation with the U.S. Air Force. He was always traveling and was seldom at his home base – Dover A.F.B.

Douglas, with his constant pursuit, soon captured my attention, and later my heart.

This would be Doug's third marriage. His parents were very worried that this marriage would also end in divorce. His mother told me that his father wept over our pending marriage.

Douglas and I married in 1960. When we got married I resigned my position as Social Studies teacher at Booker T. Washington Junior High School and moved to Brooklyn, New York to live with my husband. When I married Douglas, my weight had not yet reached 100 pounds. I stood five-foot, two inches, and wore a dress size of six or seven.

Life in Brooklyn with Douglas and Baby Leslie

In New York, with Douglas and his family and friends, I again became known as Elsie. We lived in a small kitchenette apartment on St. Mark's Place in Brooklyn until the birth of our first child, Leslie. We then moved into a four-room and single bath apartment on Hunt Avenue in Brooklyn.

My pregnancy with Leslie was a delight. This delight came from the fact that she was going to be the first baby born into the Richardson family since the birth of my baby sister, Nellie, who since deceased. My Aunt Nellie, Sis Sally and Uncle Purl in North Carolina made frequent phone calls to our home in Brooklyn to make sure all was well with me and the unborn baby. My Uncle Lee in Wildwood, New Jersey made several visits to our home to offer his assistance.

My gynecologist, Dr. Wiley Martin, was a member of Alpha Phi Alpha fraternity, as well as a long-time friend. He took very good care of me throughout my pregnancy, and delivered Leslie at Sydenham Hospital, New York City. Leslie was a healthy seven-pound baby girl. All family members were overjoyed.

I had no problem getting babysitting help for infant Leslie; both my sisters and my cousin Martha were at my beck and call. My sisters Allie and Elizabeth even volunteered to do food shopping for us.

Leslie was walking at nine months old. Her pediatrician, Dr. M. Patterson, requested that no shoes of any kind be put on her feet. She should wear socks only to allow her feet to develop normally.

Doug's father, Rev. Collins, passed away July 31, 1961. Leslie was nine months old. Douglas lost his closest friend when his father died, for it was his father's wisdom and love for his son that kept him on track most of the time. Isabelle, Douglas Jr.'s stepmother, later explained to me just how much they worried about Doug, Jr.

When she was almost twelve months old, Leslie showed signs of being allergic to something. Frequent doctor's examinations and tests led to our being informed that Leslie was allergic to pollutants in the air of New York City. Doug and I were told that the only cure for Leslie would be to move out of the city into a rural area of New York State, or another city far from the New York Metropolitan area.

Changes for Leslie's Sake

Meanwhile, our pediatrician, Dr. Patterson, suggested that our child be confined to a dust-free environment immediately to protect and preserve her respiratory-pulmonary systems. Immediately, we changed Leslie's nursery to provide the kind of dust-free environment required by Dr. Patterson. Her room was painted, her furniture, bed linen and clothing washed thoroughly, an air purifier installed in her room, and the room was sealed so that no dust could enter it. Leslie lived in this environment while Douglas and I searched for a new home far away from New York City.

Life with Doug Gets Tougher

In addition to concern and worry about the illness of our baby daughter, I had concerns about the changes in the attitude and personality of my husband. At times he was arrogant, distant and even unkind.

My two sisters, Allie and Elizabeth, were initially very excited about my marriage to Douglas. Since they did not have a brother, Douglas seemed to be just the brother they wanted and needed. They tried very hard to love and embrace him, but in retrospect, there were signs he resented our closeness from the very beginning.

Both sisters knew that I was the able educator, but not a capable cook, as they both were. Allie and Elizabeth would sometimes purchase special meats and poultry for us when they went to the Fulton Market for monthly shopping and to Jersey for vegetables. Each would also offer to cook our meat when they cooked theirs. Doug saw this as an intrusion and became angry and insulting to both Allie and Elizabeth. As far as he was concerned, communication was cut off, which forced us sisters to talk to each other when Douglas was not around.

Doug and I eventually found a place to live where the air would not be so detrimental to Leslie's health.

Doug's stepmother, Isabelle, whom we called "Nana" by then, was very satisfied with Camden, New Jersey where she had lived since the death of her husband, Rev. Collins, Doug's father. Doug and I went to Camden to search intently for a home in the upscale section of the city. We found one right across the boulevard from Nana, in the Parkside section of the city and moved there in June 1962.

Our home in Camden was located in Parkside, an exclusive neighborhood, predominantly white. Leslie, the only child at the time, had a play yard with a sand box built in it. The beautiful, brick home had six large rooms, with two floors, plus a finished knotty-pine basement. We paid extra money for custom-made drapes that matched the rugs in the living room, the dining room and the master bedroom upstairs. I was pleased that Isabelle lived across the street, almost directly in front of us. Doug, however was not pleased about this.

Leslie was almost two years old when we moved into our new home in Camden. One of the three bedrooms located upstairs was Leslie's room. The home also had a built-in children's play area, including a sandbox which offered a safe, soft play ground. Beautiful flowers and shrubbery surrounded and protected the small front patio, the side walkway and the back yard. These areas were enclosed by a wrought iron picket fence, which gave Leslie room to play outside under the watchful eyes of her parents.

At about this time, Doug was given the opportunity to serve the civil rights movement in the City of Philadelphia. The NAACP was fighting with the City of Philadelphia, pressing city officials to hire more African Americans for city jobs, including public transportation jobs. The city claimed it was unable to find qualified drivers who were not white. However, Doug was an experienced driver, and an ideal candidate to help break down the city's resistance. Doug, though, refused to cooperate with the NAACP because he would have to quit his job as a New York motorman. I was disappointed that he chose not to help with the NAACP job struggle in Philadelphia.

Shortly after moving to Camden, I was offered a teaching position in Trenton, New Jersey, which I accepted. To manage this major new responsibility, Leslie and I had to travel by bus to Trenton each Sunday afternoon. Sunday evenings and weekdays, we lived in a private rooming house owned by Miss Littlejohn, who also provided meals for us, and each Friday afternoon, after school, we traveled by bus to our home in Camden.

Doug's job with the Transit Authority meant that he would spend a great deal of time in New York during the week, staying overnight there on weekdays, but would be able to spend weekends with Leslie and me at home. Our lovely house in Camden was very often empty.

I was the teacher of Social Studies, Civics and Citizenship Education to grades 7 and 8 at Junior High School No. 5 in Trenton, New Jersey in the mid 1960's. In those years, Americans held a puritanical attitude regarding pregnant teachers in the classroom. When a teacher began to show signs of pregnancy, she was asked to resign her position. It was at this time I became pregnant with my second child, Kimberly.

The teaching arrangement continued for about seven months. On April 1, 1963, I resigned my position at the school because I was about five months pregnant, and was beginning to show with the impending arrival of my second child. Following my resignation, I went home to Camden to await the birth of my baby.

My little girl, Leslie, was excited about the prospect of having a little sister to play with. Occasionally, she would touch my stomach and carry on child-like conversations with the baby. The name Kimberly had already been decided upon by my 7th and 8th grade students in Trenton in a fun baby-naming contest. So Leslie was using the name frequently.

When I went to Cooper Hospital in Camden to deliver the baby, my sister Elizabeth and Cousin Martha Vinson came to Camden to get Leslie. They took her back to New York City and kept her for almost four weeks. When they brought her home, I was up and about and quite able to care for the children and myself.

Kimberly, like Leslie, was a pretty baby. She has copper skin tone with a head full of black curly hair. However, she had one serious problem. During the birth, her right arm was dislocated. The medical concern prompted the hospital to assign a pediatrician to care for the child and to make sure that the proper medical attention was given to the child as long as necessary. I was very concerned about her arm and wanted to make sure she was not left handicapped. I visited specialists in Philadelphia and New York City seeking the best opinions regarding the care of her arm. No one suggested an operation, but we were advised to continue the physical therapy with varying intensity.

Doug was not a participant in the therapy because he came home so very seldom at this time. Things were not going well in our marriage.

Joe and Amy Evans, my friends who lived in Philadelphia, took me to the hospital, helped me through labor, visited me and brought the baby and me home after the birth. They became Kimberly's godparents.

Leslie was the apple of her father's eye. To him, she could do no wrong. However, when the family moved to Camden, the amount of time her father spent with her, with my baby daughter Kimberly, and with me, all decreased. He did not come home regularly, as I had expected he would. However, when he was home, he and Leslie spent most of his available time together.

Leslie was a live-wire. She was always busy, either with her toys, her education materials, or "helping" her mommy. I never will forget the day she pulled a chair up to the gas stove and reached over the hot stove to pull the sterilizing baby bottles from the flame. She felt they had boiled long enough and were ready to be pulled aside. While I dressed Kimberly in the nursery, Leslie came in and announced, "Mommy, the baby's bottles are all finished, so I put them on the side." When I fully understood what she was saying, I rushed into the kitchen only to find a chair up against the stove and the baby bottle sterilizer pulled away from the fire. The fire was still on. Following this incident, Leslie and I had many conversations about the do's and don'ts of home safety. Leslie was three at the time.

I had no car, so Isabelle, Doug's mother, took me shopping and to other places as needed.

The Marriage Continues to Fail

Determined as I was to carry on with dignity, I was beginning to experience signs of distress, and weariness. My failing marriage bothered me a great deal. I searched for ways to make the marriage work, mostly blaming myself for the problems we had and trying hard to correct my "mistakes." Nothing worked, and Douglas remained very distant.

I began to shed the few pounds I had gained from carrying the children. Though I was up to 108 pounds at one point, I was now below that. My family members and friends expressed concern about my losing more weight.

By 1963, Douglas and I were separated and living apart. Mrs. Bernice Munce, Assistant Superintendent of Schools in Charge of Curriculum and Staff Development, encouraged me to return to Trenton where a job awaited me. Leslie was almost five years old when we returned to Trenton. In 1964, we sold our home in Camden.

Leslie qualified to participate in a special federal program for preschoolers. In this program of 25 hand-picked youngsters, under the direction of Mrs. Juanita Faulkner, Leslie did very well. When she was ready for kindergarten, I enrolled her. At Junior High School No. 5, where I was the seventh and eighth grade social studies teacher, the kindergarten classes were half-day. Every day Leslie and four other children were picked up by Mrs. Carter, Betty Lacey's mother, and kept until picked up by their parents. Betty Lacey was the third grade teacher at Junior No. 5, and her daughter Wanda, was also among those children picked up by Mrs. Carter, her grandmother.

Leslie simply loved school and made sure that she attended every day. Even when she did not feel well and should have stayed home, she would hide her illness in order to go to school. This early interest in school grew and enabled her to accomplish the goal of a perfect attendance record throughout her public school years; a total of thirteen years. When she graduated from Hamilton High School West, Hamilton, NJ, this accomplishment was brought to the attention of the school officials. Teachers and guidance counselors urged the officials to honor her for it would also be motivational for minority students as well. This school's officials denied her the honor of a 13-year perfect attendance award. However, the very next year, the honor was bestowed upon a white girl who had twelve years of perfect attendance.

Although Doug and I were married for twelve years, we lived apart for many of them. Still, one marvelous result of our union was two lovely, energetic daughters.

...And Life Continues Without Doug

My two daughters and I moved to Trenton in June 1964. Mrs. Munce had found us a second floor, four-room apartment in a duplex on Spring Street in Trenton. I had a job at Junior High School No. 5, teaching eight grade social studies. Because of my income level, Leslie, now 3½, qualified to participate in an experimental education program for three- and four-year-olds. This program was sponsored by the Trenton Board of Education and the federal government.

Mrs. Bessie, the lady who babysat Leslie when I taught at Junior High No. 5 in 1962, was pleased to take care of Kimberly.

By September, I was all settled in. My sisters came down from New York several times to help me get adjusted. Amy and Joe Evans, my dear friends from Philadelphia, and their two sons also came often to visit and help in whatever way they could. These individuals were a godsend.

Many Babysitters for Kimberly

In March of 1965, Miss Bessie, Kimberly's babysitter, suffered a massive heart attack and died. Kimberly had no babysitter and I did not know where to find one.

Allie and Elizabeth knew of a lady in Harlem, New York, who lived close to the poverty level with eight children at home and who was receiving welfare. They felt the family's eldest daughter, seventeen-year-old Rosie Lee, an eleventh grade student, would be a capable live-in babysitter for me and the girls. Rosie Lee would be a full-time student at Trenton Central High School, with me supervising her education. She would help me around the house, but mainly with the children. She would conduct herself as if she were my daughter. I would pay her an agreed-upon salary.

Rosie Lee agreed with the terms of this arrangement and transferred to the school system and began the program. Before the month was over,

Rosie Lee became homesick and returned home to Harlem. It was still the month of March.

A young woman named Odell was then recommended to me as a possible babysitter. She was a distant cousin of an acquaintance of mine and needed a job. I interviewed Odell, found her to be capable and trustworthy and hired her to baby-sit Kimberly, play with her, take her outside for walks and play, feed her lunch and have her take an afternoon nap. School was out for me at 3:30 p.m. and I would be home by 4:00 p .m. Odell would be able to leave shortly after 4:00 p.m. All went well and I was mostly satisfied with what seemed to be a fairly good job done.

Then one morning, I was called into the principal's office. Mr. Smith, the principal, told me to go home and look after my child. He said that he would assign someone to take over my class for the rest of the day. My heart was in my mouth and I practically ran all the way home. The distance was about one mile from Montgomery Street to Spring Street where I lived.

When I arrived home, I found my home fully occupied with people who were friends of Odell. They were scattered through the home socializing and hanging out. Odell was busy cooking food for her friends. Kimberly was ignored.

When I arrived, Odell got the surprise of her life. The party was over and she was fired. It was the end of April and school would not be over until the first week of June. I needed a babysitter for the month of May and one week in June. School would then be out for the summer and I could search for a more permanent babysitter.

About four blocks north on Spring Street, where we were, lived a pleasant couple with three children. Two of the children were in school and the mother was at home with the baby. I made up my mind to ask this couple to please keep Kimberly during the day for the next five weeks until school closed. I pleaded with them and finally won their sympathy. Kimberly was in good hands.

Both Leslie and Kimberly were alert and advanced for their ages. I spent a good amount of time talking with them and training them. They were potty-trained early and they walked and talked early: Leslie at nine months, and Kimberly at about ten months.

Leslie was doing well in the pre-school program with Ms. Juanita, her teacher, and the other 19 or 20 little boys and girls in her class.

Kimberly turned two years old on July 29. School was out, and I knew that during the summer, I would have to find a babysitter for Kimberly once again.

A Nursery School and Friends Ease My Burdens

A couple of blocks from Spring Street, on the corner of Bellevue and Calhoun Street was the Corner Day Nursery School. It was owned and operated by the Bray family. I felt that it would be wonderful if I could enroll Kimberly in this nursery school. I went to talk with Mrs. Bray, the owner and teacher about that possibility. There was a long waiting list, but the major problem was Kimberly's age. State law required that all children attending nursery school had to be two and a half years old. Kim had just turned two, but she met with flying colors all the other requirements, such as being potty trained, able to feed herself, and able to leave mom and play independently. But Kim would have to wait until January, right after Christmas, before she could be enrolled.

Mrs. Bray felt sorry for me for she knew how difficult it was to find decent childcare, so she made a bargain with me. She would admit Kimberly to the daily program at Corner Day, but would not register her. Her name would not appear on anything, but she would be an active participant in the program. Of course, I would pay the required weekly fee just as other parents did. If the inspectors or supervisors asked about "that" child, Mrs. Bray would say that Kim is her grandchild. I was overjoyed and most grateful. Kim began her nursery school program at Corner Day and was picked up and delivered daily by Uncle Donny. Kimberly loved her school.

Around this time, I had made two other important, and kind, male friends: Reilly Crews and Coleridge Matthews. In both cases, it was a friendship, not a love affair. Between the two of them, I was able to do my major food shopping and take care of other business where a car was necessary.

Shortly after school ended for summer vacation in 1966, Mr. Bob Johnson, my landlord, came to me and said that he wanted me out of the apartment in two weeks. The reason was not made clear. This did not make sense to me, but I knew that I had to move out of that apartment.

After looking for an apartment for a few weeks with Reilly and Coleridge, crisscrossing the city, I located a place just two blocks down the street from where I then lived. Owned by a widow who lived in Princeton, New Jersey, it was a five-room, first-floor apartment. I took it, and with the help of my friends and family, we moved in during August of 1966. Because this apartment was larger than the one from which we just moved, I purchased additional materials and items to decorate the home to my satisfaction. Our little family of three was happy for the time being.

However, the landlady turned out to be especially unpleasant. She often came to the house, finding fault and giving orders. Eventually, she told me that she was unhappy with my presence and wanted me out of the house within a few months. Twice within a few months, I was asked to move.

Again, I was out looking for an apartment. Many of my friends were also helping me look for an apartment. Then one day at school, Bernice Hunt, sixth grade teacher at Junior No. 5, where I also taught, told me about the housing complex where she and her family lived. The complex was called South Olden Apartments, Inc., located on Arena Drive in Hamilton Township. She said that they are new apartments and were barely rented. She urged me to contact the rental office as soon as possible.

I took Bernice's suggestion to call. I was invited out for an interview and to file an application. My application was accepted, and we were able to move into the new apartment on May 1, 1967.

After we moved, I made arrangements with Bernice to ride with her to school each day. I then bought myself a car and learned to drive under her supervision. I soon became the principal driver to school.

As the children grew older and my economic situation changed, so did Doug's financial responsibilities to his family. Both Kimberly and Leslie attended parochial school for their elementary education. They attended Bethany Lutheran Grammar School in Ewing, New Jersey. Leslie attended grades one through six, and Kimberly attended Kindergarten through third. Both took dancing lessons and learned tap, jazz and ballet. They also took piano lessons. Leslie learned to play the piano particularly well.

Doug did not give up his quest to bring me pain and humiliation. He began to journey to Hamilton Township in search of individuals he could talk to about me. He thought he had found a good candidate when he met Augustus (Gus) Hunt, Bernice's husband. One evening he invited himself over to their home with some urgent news to tell them. Gus invited him in. Doug proceeded to tell Gus that I was a bad influence for his wife. Gus became so angry with Doug that he cut him off during the conversation, opened the front door and asked Doug to leave and never return. Before closing the door, he lectured Doug about just how low a man had to be to talk about his wife, the mother of his children, in such a manner. Doug went on his way.

Immediately afterward, Gus called me and asked if he could talk with me in my home. He said he had something very important to tell me. After he came over and described what happened, I continued to worry about Doug destroying my reputation, something he had attempted in the past.

Finally Divorced

I finally decided to divorce Doug. For years he had threatened me with the idea, but never took steps to do so. I was truly fed up with his actions and took the necessary steps to divorce him. After twelve years of marriage, our divorce became final in 1972.

The lawyer proved mental cruelty and family abandonment. Therefore, the bulk of the cost was paid by Doug, and I paid only $200. Doug and I were awarded joint custody of the children, and they were allowed to spend a great deal of time with their father in Mt. Vernon, where he lived. Because the children were so young (eight and five), I was always quite worried when they spent weeks or weekends with their father in Mt. Vernon. I suspected that he left them alone all day while he traveled to New York City to work.

Although Doug may have been assigned definite hours to work, his job with the New York Transit Authority required that he be available to report to work at any time of the day or night. This work responsibility made it quite difficult for him to properly supervise his two young daughters. It was discovered later that in this case, he left them alone, often, after being called for emergency duty at the subway system. This had put the children in serious danger. It was precisely on one of these occasions that a social worker entered the home where he had a room and found the children in the house alone. The State of New Jersey was contacted, the proper authorities got involved, and Doug lost shared custody of the children. He could visit them at their home, on designated weekends, but could not take them away. He became quite angry about this arrangement.

Following the divorce, others, as well as myself, noticed that Doug became more attentive to his family. He began to visit more and called often. He even talked to me. "His love came down" was the popular expression people used to refer to his changed attitude. In 1973, one year after the divorce, he posed a question that stunned me. He asked me to remarry him, claiming that he realized he had made a mistake over the years by mistreating me. He insisted that he had changed. By that point, I was not at all interested in marriage, so I rejected the offer.

Doug continued his pursuit, and was very attentive to the children, who were now pre-teens. By this time, I had become an assistant professor at the local teachers college. In 1975, he once again asked me to remarry him. He said that we would move to Mt. Vernon. He wanted me to pick out the house I wanted and its location in Mt. Vernon. He stated that he had saved enough money to provide a beautiful home for his family. There was one caveat. He expected me to resign my position at Trenton State College, remarry him and move to Mt. Vernon.

I was not interested. My love for Douglas was gone, and I did not trust him. And, just as importantly, I now had a secure position at Trenton State College, and loved my work.

If I had remarried Doug, it is doubtful I would have achieved all I did, including my rising career and advanced studies in the field of education.

Note: *An extensive discussion about my children may be found in the next sections of this book.*

A Notepad of my Musical Experiences – Solos and Choral Involvement

Titles of Selections	Author/Arranger
Italian Street Song	Victor Herbert
Lamb of God – Agnus Dei	
Sanctus (solo part in Latin)	Gounod
Seek ye the Lord	Dr. J.U. Roberts
Hallelujah Chorus	G.F. Handel
He Shall Feed His Flock	G. F. Handel
Ave Marie (solo)	Franz Schubert
(Alleluia) Alleluia (solo)	W. A. Mozart
"Je dis que rien ne m'epouilante" from Carmen (soprano solo)	George Bizet
Ma Lindy Lou	Lily Strickland
"Obstination" "A Resolve"	H. de Fontenailles
The Lord's Prayer	Albert Hay Molotte
Because	Guy d'Hardelot
Will You Remember "Sweetheart"	Sigmund Romberg
City Called Heaven	Hall Johnson
O Divine Redeemer	Charles Gounod
I Know that My Redeemer Liveth	G. F. Handel
Finest Album of Religious Songs	Paul LaBerte compilation
The Psalms	
Bless This House	
Wings	
The Swan	
Sweet Little Jesus Boy	Negro Spiritual
Without a Song	
(Life) I Love Life	
Somebody's Knocking at Your Door	Negro Spiritual

Steal Away	Negro Spiritual
Amazing Grace	Negro Spiritual
Oh Danny Boy	
Were You There	Negro Spiritual
Where'er Ye Walk	
My Lord What Morning	Negro Spiritual
Good News Chariot's Coming	Negro Spiritual
The Seven Last Words of Christ	Theodore DuBois
A Sacred Cantata – *contains many solos*	

Choral Selections – Professor and Choral Director

1. Our Musical Heritage – 1951 Columbia University	Harry Robert Wilson, Conductor
2. Choral Collection Summer Session – 1952 Columbia University	Harry Robert Wilson, Conductor Travis Sheldon, Assistant Conductor
3. Choral Collection, Summer Session – 1953 Columbia University	Harry Robert Wilson, Conductor Travis Sheldon, Assistant Conductor
4. Choral Collection, Summer Session – 1954 Columbia University	Harry Robert Wilson, Conductor Travis Sheldon, Assistant Conductor Robert Oldham, Accompanist
5. Great Hymns Mass Choir Member Delaware Conference	Director: Rev. Dr. Daniel Ridout, District Superintendent, South Jersey/ Delaware Conference, Methodist Episcopal Church
6. Choral Society of Greater Trenton Trenton, NJ; Ewing, NJ; Lawrence, NJ; Princeton, NJ; and New York City, NY	Director: Charles L. D. Higgins, Princeton, New Jersey

Concerts/Selections

Magnificat	Johann S. Bach
Anthems from Scripture	Clifford McCormick
The Messiah	G.F. Handel
Psalms of Joy	Boosey & Hawkes
Upon This Rock	Harry Robert Wilson
Symphonies de Psoumes	Igor Stravinsky
Zoltan Kodaly "Te Deum"	
Sleepers, Wake I	J. S. Bach
J. S. Bach Choral Works	J. S. Bach
Missa Solemnis in D	Ludwig Von Beethoven
Requiem	Brahms
Requiem	Verdi
Requiem	Mozart

Setbacks and Successes for My Daughters

Leslie Jean and Kimberly Ruth Go to School and Experience Life

When my divorce from Douglas became final in 1972, Leslie was twelve years old and Kimberly was nine. At that point, Douglas and I had not lived together as a couple for many years. Our two daughters lived with me in Trenton, New Jersey and Douglas visited them at his leisure. However, following the divorce, the lawyer established definite visitation schedules/rights for Douglas that were adhered to.

The girls and I were snug in a two bedroom apartment in a cooperative housing unit built by the federal government for middle class Americans. We had a corner apartment where the playground was close to the house, so that I could very easily supervise the children when they were at play.

Being a single parent had its challenges. Providing the best care possible for my children was my first priority. Since my plate was full with work, childcare and home responsibilities, I decided to pare down certain activities to be sure to take care of the necessities.

I cut back my social life and many of my social connections. I told Mrs. Munce that I was unable to join the organization called The Links; I became unfinancial in Alpha Kappa Alpha Sorority; and I rarely attended meetings of the Education Sorority of Phi Delta Kappa. On the other hand, I maintained my involvement with my church, St. Paul

United Methodist. Elizabeth Campbell and I became Director of the Youth Program; I was a member of the Chancel Choir and Choir Soloist, as well. Over the years, involvement in church work became more extensive. I was appointed chair of the Missions Program, representative to Trenton Ecumenical Area Ministry (TEAM), a member of Education Department, member of the Board of Directors for the After School Latch Key Program for St. Paul, and became an Administrative Board member and coordinator of Vacation Bible School. Both Leslie and Kimberly were becoming involved in church programs and activities as their ages and interests dictated.

Leslie and Kimberly did not attend the elementary school in the Hamilton Public School System. There were heavy demands made upon my time by my position at the college. Also, there was to be considered the girls' need of a supervisor before leaving for school and after returning home from schools. They would have to walk to school each day because of the location of their home. I decided to put them in parochial school to address these concerns and meet the special needs of the girls. Bethany Lutheran Grammar School became the answer for us.

Bethany is located on Parkside Boulevard, Ewing, New Jersey. Its location allowed me to drop the girls off on my way to work. Paying the tuition bill for the two required certain adjustments. I am proud to say I was able to put the two girls in parochial school. Leslie began first grade at about age five, and Kimberly at two and a half, was enrolled in the Day Care Program at Bethany.

At Bethany, Leslie was involved in the activities that the school offered, which included drama, Glee Club, and a few sports. Leslie loved school, was very popular and maintained perfect attendance. She was also the youngest student in her class. She completed her entire elementary program at Bethany, after which I enrolled her in the Grice Middle School, a public school in Hamilton.

Leslie Shows Promise, But Faces Racism

At Grice School, Leslie also found herself a friend who became her protector and ally. His name was Tommy and he lived in the Hamilton Parks Apartments where we lived. Tommy was Italian, and two years Leslie's senior. He lived with his parents, who were business people, and a brother, who was two years ahead of Tommy in school. Tommy would step up and prevent racial harassment and bullying that often occurred on the school bus against minority students. Even at school, Leslie had protection because Tommy was so well respected.

Leslie began to form friendships in middle school that she carried throughout her senior high years. She joined the swimming team, the soccer team, and the color guard of the marching band in extracurricular activities, excelling in all areas.

Other Successes for Leslie

Leslie was also invited to become a member of a small dance group formed by Miss Isabel Stewart Johnson, a capable dance instructor. Because of rehearsal schedule time and days, plus the distance from home to rehearsals, I was unable to meet expectations of the dance instructor. Leslie was quite disappointed when she had to drop out.

Leslie was very good in art, especially drawing. She and her girlfriend drew, knitted and crocheted a beautiful piece of art work that caught the attention of every one who saw it. The school tried to take it and hang it in the library to become school property. The parents of the two girls objected, and the art was returned to the girls.

Mr. David Carroll came to the house and gave the girls piano lessons for about ten years. Kimberly became disinterested and gave up the piano after a few years, but Leslie continued and was able to finally play the piano.

When Leslie turned fifteen years old, she got her working papers and landed her first job at Rustler's Restaurant in Hamilton. I allowed this but we agreed on the following terms: She could work not more than two hours per day cleaning tables, and she would never work past 10:00 on any night. I always transported Leslie and did not allow her to ride with others. This was one of the many successful employment experiences for Leslie, including three summers working with children at East Trenton Day Care Center, and a stint as assistant to the director of Hamilton Square United Methodist Church's Vacation Bible School. Her supervisors were deeply impressed by Leslie's talents.

By the time Leslie became a senior, all of her closest girlfriends were white. One little girl, whose name was Helen, lived alone with her father in Hamilton Township. She considered Leslie to be one of her best friends and always wanted Leslie to spend the night with her. I had concerns with Leslie spending the night with Helen, but I would let her spend some Saturday afternoons playing with Helen at her home. I knew that Helen's father was seldom home.

Meeting Expectations

One of Leslie's classmates held a midnight swimming party one Saturday night and Leslie was invited. I thoroughly discussed the pros and cons of such a party with Leslie, for I was not keen about allowing her to attend. I finally agreed, providing the following rules were followed: 1) I would take her; 2) I would remain at the party; and 3) I would bring Leslie home from the party at 2:00 a.m.. The rules were accepted, so Kimberly (age 12) and I attended the swim party at midnight. I was among two other parents who attended. At 2:00 a.m., sixteen-year-old Leslie left the party with her sister Kimberly and me. Refreshments had not yet been served, but the guests were drinking ice cold beer that was made available to everyone.

Leslie's interest in school remained high into her senior year. She pursued a solid academic program throughout high school with special interest in math and science.

Throughout her years in middle and senior high school, Leslie maintained perfect school attendance.

In a graduating class of 459 students, Leslie graduated number 59 in her class at age seventeen.

Leslie received a science fellowship to attend Delaware State College and joined a group of 20 carefully selected students who began the studies the summer prior to the opening of school in September. Upon graduation from Hamilton West, the guidance counselors at both Grice Middle School and Hamilton West High School, discovered that Leslie had maintained a perfect attendance record throughout her education. It was so unbelievable that a very careful check was ordered by the Director of Secondary Education of the school district. The record held. Leslie had spent thirteen years in school, beginning with kindergarten, and had maintained a perfect attendance. I felt that Leslie's dedication ought to be recognized, but the school district of Hamilton would not accept these facts and decided against the recognition of such an accomplishment. Leslie was quite disappointed. I put up quite a fight to have Leslie recognized for such an accomplishment, but the administration refused. Many agreed with me that Leslie's race was the deciding factor.

The Hamilton High School marching band became recognized among the top marching bands in the United States. It performed in many special events in states in eastern U.S.A., including Florida. Among the highlights of its travel was a trip to Bermuda to perform. The routines performed by the Color Guard were one of the great highlights.

Leslie, like Kimberly, had taken dancing lessons since she was four years old. Now, she was quite an agile dancer, and danced annually in the culminating activities at the War Memorial Building in Trenton, New Jersey. She was so good in her dance routine as a color guard member, that the girls voted her to be their leader, the premiere of the color guards in senior high school. This meant that Leslie would be featured independently in routines at all major functions in addition to being the leader of the color guard, whenever, and wherever they marched. But this was not to be.

When the parents of the girls in the color guard learned that Leslie was African American, they protested to the school. Leslie's opportunity to serve in this leadership office was denied. She asked me not to intervene, so I did not. As a consolation, she was given the number one position in the color guard line, and would lead the line. Leslie was deeply hurt by the school's decision to knuckle under to pressure from a group of racist parents and disregard the request of her color guard peers, but her self-discipline and belief in herself enabled her to carry on.

Leslie maintained her self-control. I protested to the school administration and to the Physical Education Director about the denial of the students' wishes, but received no cooperation from them. Leslie was also a member of the famous Black Hawk Marching Band.

My own inner strength, self-discipline, personal and family goals and religious beliefs were definitely passed down to my daughters. I spent a great deal of family time talking to them about the ultimate goal, which was the accomplishment of their own personal goals, and that they must never allow anyone to derail them. They were told never to begin a disturbance or a fight, but rather find a reason to walk away from trouble. But, if someone hits or strikes them, I taught them they could hit them back, then leave the scene. Call Momma and go home, if possible. But by all means, leave that scene.

Off to College

Leslie spent four years at Delaware State College and graduated with a B.S. degree in Math in 1983. John (Jack) Wilson, a member of St. Paul United Methodist Church, was Vice President, New York Life Insurance Company. Jack paved the way for Leslie to gain employment at this esteemed insurance company the year of her graduation. She spent several years at New York Life. Her skill, know-how, and dedication did not go unnoticed. She was soon asked to become a member of an independent three-person group. She was interested in the opportunity, but felt she needed to talk at length about this opportunity with her mother. I encouraged her to make a decision based on what she knew about the other two people in the business, and the insurance business itself. Leslie decided she would join the group and give it her best shot.

After two years of extensive work, I could see the strain on her. Fieldwork by day and long late hours at night were beginning to take its toll on Leslie, and I was very concerned. I encouraged Leslie to take a vacation and come home to Trenton for some much needed rest. Leslie went even further; she resigned from the insurance group and came home. She knew she would have no trouble finding work in the insurance field. She had extensive, in-depth experience in the business from the beginning level to aspects of management. She had also taken all the courses required by the insurance business of New York State over a period of ten years, and was certified to practice insurance in New York, New Jersey, and Connecticut.

Meanwhile, Delaware State College offered Leslie a stipend to do graduate studies in the area of math and science. After a year and one-half to two years of study, she would receive a master's degree in math.

Leslie moved into my house on McKee Road in Dover, Delaware. There she relaxed while she mulled over her future plans and decided which courses to take. During this period she met Daniel Morgan Ramsey. The two had nearly an instant attraction for each other, but did not make any plans immediately to cultivate the friendship. Leslie decided against accepting the stipend to attend Delaware State for a master's degree, but instead accepted a job position in the Department of Insurance for the State of Delaware.

Leslie Gets Married

Friendship between Leslie and Dan, who is white, developed into love. They became engaged and announced that their wedding would take place in two years. They moved in together and began to work out very elaborate wedding plans. I was invited to become very involved in the planning and the execution of the plans, and so was Janis, Dan's mother.

The marriage presented a problem to some in the Ramsey family members because it was an interracial union. When it became apparent that this couple's plans were not going to be derailed, Dan's parents, plus the majority of his siblings, supported the marriage.

I helped plan a beautiful wedding at St. Paul United Methodist Church in Trenton, on September 23, 1995. Cassidy, their oldest daughter was born a year later and Macy, the younger daughter was born three years later. As I write this, the family lives in an upscale neighborhood called Grand Oaks, Dover, Delaware. Both Dan and Leslie work for the State of Delaware. Dan is coordinator, Department of Purchasing and Distribution of Services. Leslie is coordinator, Department of Personnel Services.

Kim Faces Racism; I Confront School Leaders

Once Leslie graduated from Bethany Elementary School, Kimberly was no longer interested in remaining there without her sister. She also wanted to attend Hamilton Schools. I transferred Kimberly and enrolled her in Holmdel Elementary School in the Hamilton district. She entered the fourth grade there. I arranged my schedule so that I would be able to drive Kimberly to school daily, and be at home when both she and Leslie returned each day. Leslie rode the bus to school daily, but arrived home at about the same time that Kimberly did. She was a seventh grader, and Kimberly was in fourth grade.

Kimberly's fourth grade teacher at Holmdel School became unhappy with the presence of a black child in her class, so she decided to set up a segregated classroom. The Holmdel School population was 100% white at the time Kimberly enrolled. Her presence was both resented and rejected by her teacher and her classmates, which caused Kimberly to raise many questions to her mom about this conduct.

Both Kimberly and Leslie were quite familiar with an integrated society. Most of their friends were white because that was the working and religious world in which they lived. Trenton State College, where I worked, is a predominantly white college, our church is a largely white United Methodist Church, Bethany is a predominantly white parochial school, and Hamilton Park, where we lived is a predominantly white housing complex, and the schools are predominantly white. So living among white people is a way of life for the girls. Still, Kimberly was treated as an outcast at Holmdel School.

The fourth grade teacher to whom Kimberly was assigned separated her students by race, which meant, as the only black youngster in class, my child was isolated. Kimberly was very confused about this arrangement. She continuously asked me why she had to sit by herself. I soon realized what was up and decided to visit the school to see for myself.

The teacher had created a segregated classroom. Twenty white children sat on one side of the room and one black child, my Kimberly, sat on the other side of the room. I reported the problem to the school principal and the supervisor of elementary education for Hamilton School System. They failed to concede the need for action and the situation continued. I then got in touch with a lawyer who in turn contacted the Division of Civil Rights. A suit was filed against the Hamilton Township School System. The charge was "discrimination against an African American Student." The charge hit the news media (television, newspapers and radio), which shook up the Board of Education.

The media spotlight was too much for the township to handle. Changes were made immediately and the news went to all citizens. Soon the situation changed at the school and Kimberly was treated with respect by all. I, too, was respected but not necessarily liked, by the "powers that be."

The girls did well in school. I made sure that they pursued ambitious academic programs because they were both capable and quite bright.

Another Obstacle for Kim

When Kimberly completed elementary school at Holmdel, she was enrolled at Grice Middle School, where Leslie was in attendance. Before school opened that September, I received a letter from the Reading Supervisor of the school district. This letter informed me that Kimberly would be placed in a remedial reading class, and that a meeting was being called by her reading teacher and that I was expected to be in attendance. I immediately contacted a friend of mine, Dr. O'Connor, a psychologist, and discussed this concern with him. Dr. O'Connor suggested that an independent school psychologist test Kimberly, prior to the school's testing program, which was required of all students in remedial programs. It was further suggested that he would take the test results and deal directly with the school system. These steps cost me a great deal of money, but it was well worth it.

Kimberly was given a battery of tests by a prominent school psychologist prior to the opening of school. She scored extremely high on all aspects of the test. She was reading three grade levels ahead of her class. She also had an IQ measured as 125. Kimberly was placed in a straight academic track at Grice and continued on this track through high school at Hamilton High West. She graduated from high school with a strong academic background.

Kimberly was involved in extracurricular activities throughout middle and senior high school. At Grice she was a member of the soccer team and she became a fairly good player. During the second year on the team, she was hit by the ball, which caused a portion of skin from her thigh to become separated from her leg. She was out of school for six weeks and received "home instruction."

Kim Becomes a Mother

Kimberly was also a member of the drama club and swimming club. When Kimberly entered Hamilton High School West, she continued her involvement in the drama club and appeared in several school plays. She was quite good at acting. Shortly after graduating from high school she fell in love with a young man whose name was Roland Hunter. She became impregnated by him and gave birth to a little baby girl. She was given the name of Melody Tramaine Hunter. Kimberly was nineteen years old. I gained custody of Melody, giving Kimberly the financial and family support she needed. Since Roland was an inconsistent father figure, I advised Kimberly not to marry him. She followed my advice.

Kimberly's Nursing Career

Kimberly was always interested in helping people, so she decided she wanted to become a nurse. From age 12 through 15 Kimberly worked at Helene Fuld Hospital as a Junior Hospital Volunteer (Candy Striper). I enrolled her in the two-year registered nursing program at Mercer County Community College in September, following her graduation from high school. I later learned that a counselor at the Community College persuaded most of those girls in that class to withdraw from the college and take the one-year nursing class at the technical high school and become a Licensed Practical Nurse. Kimberly withdrew along with some other young students and enrolled. I lost all the first semester money paid to the community college. One year later, Kimberly was an L.P.N..

For quite a few years after graduation, Kim worked as a private nurse in Mercer County. But she soon became restless and decided she would join our relatives in Goldsboro, North Carolina and work in the hospitals in that city. She contacted my Aunt May Bell, who invited her to stay with her while she applied for a position several hospitals in Goldsboro.

Kimberly and I appeared before Judge Wilson Noden who returned custody of Melody to Kimberly when Melody was five years old and Kimberly 23. Kim packed up her clothes and belongings and my granddaughter, Melody, and drove from Trenton to Goldsboro, North Carolina. I was anxious and worried about their safety on this trip, just the two of them, but I gave them my blessings and some money. They arrived safe and sound and called to reassure me.

Kimberly was able to get a job as an LPN at Cherry Hospital right away. She also made many friends in Goldsboro, one of which was Faye, who was very supportive and became her right hand buddy.

Kimberly had developed into a very attractive young woman. She was tall, medium build, copper brown complexion, long black hair, quite shapely, and very smart. She was a very popular young woman.

Kim also had a business sense about her, so she decided that she would buy a house in Goldsboro and live there. When she told me about her idea, I wanted to be involved in the business arrangements so that the real estate agencies would not take advantage of her. I also hired a lawyer to assist her. Kim bought the house in a very upscale section of Goldsboro and moved in. After the academic year ended and my summer teaching duties were finished, I went to Goldsboro to spend the rest of the summer helping Kim furnish her home.

Before her twenty-fourth birthday, Kim met Aubrey C. Myers, Sr., a Master Sergeant and career person in the U.S. Air Force. She fell in love with him. Aubrey, eight years her senior, was divorced and had three small sons at home, ages 11, 8 and 7.

A few months after their meeting, Aubrey was deployed to Elmendorf Air Force Base in Anchorage, Alaska. He asked Kimberly to go with him. Kimberly was filled with excitement and told Aubrey she would be happy to accompany him and his sons to Alaska.

A few days later, she called me in Trenton and told me of her plans. I was stunned. Alaska is so far away and Aubrey so new to her. I objected to such a move at this time and begged my daughter not to go, but she was determined to do so. She turned over the rental and management of her house to a real estate agency. She and Melody went with Aubrey and his sons to Alaska. The care and supervision of the house was neglected, which prompted Kim to sell it years later at a considerable loss.

Off to Alaska

The newly merged family moved into a large house on the Elmendorf Air Force Base and settled down. Kimberly and I spoke often by phone, and I became content that all was well with this family. However, about eight months later, that changed. The family had broken up. Aubrey and his boys moved out of the house to another section of the base. Kimberly was alone, jobless, and homeless with a five-year-old daughter in Alaska.

I panicked. All the images of the homeless rushed to mind and I felt helpless. Meanwhile, because Kimberly could not live in base housing, she had to move. At the time of the phone call, she and Melody were temporarily housed in the shelter for the homeless. I advised her to get in touch with the Division of Family Services immediately, tell them about her predicament, and ask for help. Kimberly did this and she and Melody were put into a small apartment that cost $350 per month. I paid the first two months rent. Kim soon discovered that she was pregnant with twins, which required an increase in the aid she received from the State of Alaska. The twins (Alexis and Aubrey) were born September 13, 1989 and soon after, the small family moved into a larger apartment. The Division of Family Services paid most of the rent, and I paid the balance, and I continued to help Kimberly in various ways from thousands of miles away and for an extended period of time.

Sgt. Aubrey Myers, Sr. and his sons played no role in the lives of the twins. He and Kimberly cut off communication with each other entirely. However, my role in their lives increased. Kimberly decided to return to college and complete a four-year degree in the field of nursing. The State of Alaska is very rich in natural resources. Therefore, many exceptional opportunities are given to its citizens. A college education is almost free. With the help of federal grants (Pell, for example), she was not burdened with a large loan. She enrolled at the University of Alaska at Anchorage, which offered her substantial financial aid.

My role in helping to care for the children increased. Kimberly came to New Jersey during the summer, prepared to leave one of the twins with me. She left Alexis, who was ten months old and not quite walking. Alexis stayed with me for the next year.

The next September, Kim brought Aubrey Jr. to stay with "Mimi," but returned during the Christmas holidays and took both the twins back to Alaska with her. They were two years old.

The twins' birthday fell after the cut-off date for enrollment in school in Alaska, which is July 1st. To make sure that they were not a year behind their classmates, it was decided to enroll the twins in Kindergarten in New Jersey, where the cut-off date for school enrollment is October 30th.

When the twins were four years old, they were brought to Trenton to spend almost a year with me. They were enrolled in the Miriam Morris Private Day School in Hamilton Township, at the cost of $600 per month, where they spent the spring, summer and fall months. When school opened in September, they, like all the other students, were enrolled into kindergarten. They turned five September 13th. During the Thanksgiving break from school, Kimberly returned them to Alaska. Their school records were then transferred from New Jersey to Alaska, and they were rightfully enrolled in the Alaska School System.

Melody was also in school and was doing quite well. Alaska is a well-endowed state and does not hesitate to provide many extracurricular activities in schools throughout the state. Melody was involved in many activities such as modeling, travel, acting, sports, receiving in-depth educational experience from kindergarten through sixth grade.

Kimberly continued her studies at the University of Alaska and graduated with a B.S. degree in Nursing Services.

Kimberly Gets Married

Aubrey Sr. and Kimberly had rekindled their relationship, and planned their wedding for 1993. Aubrey had been transferred from Elmendorf Air Force Base in Alaska to Langley Air Force Base in Norfolk, Virginia; but Kimberly remained in Alaska where she worked part-time in the Sisters of Providence Hospital.

Kimberly and Aubrey exchanged nuptial vows at the Seymour Johnson Air Force Base in Goldsboro on June 10, 1993. They remained at the Langley Air Force Base until Aubrey was assigned to duty at the Pentagon in Washington, D.C.. The family then moved to Woodbridge, Virginia to be near Aubrey's assignment. Soon after, having served 23 years in the U.S. Air Force, Aubrey retired. Since their wedding, they have been blessed with two more additions to the family; Albany was born in 1997 and Amari was born in 2002. The family now lives in Yorktown, Virginia.

Recalling Vacations with My Daughters and Other Fun Times

It was my policy to always spend planned vacation time with the girls every year. This vacation time came in the summer after my job of teaching summer school at The College of New Jersey (formerly Trenton State College) was over. Usually it was during the first few weeks in August.

One of the places we usually visited was Wildwood, New Jersey. My Uncle Lee and Aunt Anna had a charming house in Wildwood, and they constantly encouraged the girls and me to spend time with them. Since Wildwood is only 125 miles southeast of Trenton, we drove down on several occasions to spend time enjoying the excitement and beach.

I also had the girls, who were under ten years old in the late 1960's, visit Wilson's Mills, the small town where I grew up. Bro Purl, Cousin Ione and her sister Cousin Jessie were always delighted when the girls came to visit; especially Bro Purl who adored both girls. Since Ione did not pass away until 1993, the girls got to know her quite well. In their teenage years, I brought them to Wilson's Mills often to visit relatives. Leslie spent three weeks with Ione one summer.

For three consecutive summers, my pre-teen girls attended the YMCA Summer camp. When they reached the proper age, they were also among the children hand-picked to participate in the Trenton State College six-week summer school education program. I was one of the professors conducting the program. The children participating in this program were the sons and daughters of professors, business executives, doctors and other especially bright students recommended by the participating schools. Both girls continued to be participants in the program until they outgrew it.

Christmas and New Year's were fun filled times to which the family looked forward. Everyone was out of school; the girls for two weeks and I for one month for the college always closed for the month of January. Nana (Isabelle Collins, Douglas's stepmother) always spent Christmas week with us.

Christmas Day at my friends Amy and Joe's in Yeadon, Pennsylvania was a highlight. Early Christmas morning, the girls and I drove to Camden, New Jersey and picked up Nana. We then crossed the Benjamin Franklin Bridge into Philadelphia and drove through the city to Yeadon, Pennsylvania. There we spent the entire day and well into the night with Amy, Joe and family members and friends enjoying a feast, playing games, exchanging gifts and celebrating the birth of Christ. When we returned home to Trenton, it was early morning of the next day. This celebration at Amy and Joe's continued close to fifteen years, and ended when Amy's diabetes became severe and caused her death in 1993. Joe passed away of a massive heart attack three years later in 1996.

Also during the Christmas break, Allie and her two younger children, Teresa and Willie, would spend a few days with us in Trenton. Aunt Anna and Uncle Lee spent time visiting with us in Trenton, too.

Annually, we would spend part of the Easter break in Teaneck with my sister Allie, her husband Jimmie and their children. During these visits the young people visited New York City, took in a show at Radio City Music Hall, and attended The Church on the Hill, Allie and Jimmy's church.

The girls also spent supervised summer vacation time and designated weekends with their father. At one point I became upset when I learned that he allowed them to sit in their folding chairs along the banks of a treacherous part of the Delaware River to fish. I stopped it immediately. Their subsequent fishing experiences were changed to a safer area of the river or another river, altogether.

Leslie became a volunteer for Vacation Bible School, Presbyterian Church, Hamilton Square one summer when she was fifteen. When she was sixteen she became a regular worker at the East Trenton Day Care Center. Kimberly was a candy striper at the Helene Fuld Hospital in Trenton from age 12 to 14.

Both daughters now have college degrees and both are professionally employed in their chosen field. Each has married and lives with their family in different states. Leslie is married to Daniel M. Ramsey and they have two lovely daughters: Cassidy Ellen and Macy Grayson in Dover, Delaware. Kimberly is married to Aubrey C. Myers, Sr. and they have four children and four blended children. They are Alexis Allie, Aubrey, Jr., Albany Ro-Elle, and Amari Elsie, The blended children are Melody Tramaine, Kwaine Aubrey, Demetri Christopher, and Jayson. The blended children are now young adults who have their own careers, and do not live at home.

My Other Jobs, Education, Experience and Community Involvement

I began my working career at fifteen, which was the legal age for youngsters in the State of New York. As usual, Allie and I were spending the summer months with our parents in Jamaica, New York. In the south, where my sisters and I lived with our grandparents, school closed in May. Just as soon as school closed, both Allie and I were on the train coming to New York to live with our parents, where we remained until mid-September.

At 15, I was old enough to have a summer job and earn some money. My parents promised me that I could spend all the money on myself to buy my own school clothes. I was delighted. I knew that I would do well working the entire summer since we did not return south until mid-September. I could work June, July, August and half of September and make a lot of money for school.

The only job I could get was a sleep-in job as a mother's helper. My responsibilities were to take care of the children, or child, while the mother carried out the responsibilities of home management. I was expected to clean up the kitchen, dining area, and wash the dishes. I would also bathe the children, put them to bed and retire to my room. For this continuous responsibility, I received \$25-\$30 per month. The time frame was the mid-1930's.

My real first job turned out to be a disaster for me. The job was located in Laurelton, New York, a distance from my parents. My mother was unhappy about the distance from home, as well as being skeptical about the uncertainty expressed by the madam of the house regarding my ability to handle the responsibilities. I was allowed to try it out, but would be removed from the job if it became too demanding.

Indeed it was demanding. At fifteen, I became a full-time maid caring for three children, instead of the one as claimed by the parent. I kept the entire house clean, washed several times per week for a family of five, did the ironing, including the husband's shirts. When I saw my parents on Thursdays and every other Sunday, I must have appeared very tired and drawn. They felt that it was time for me to quit even though it had only been a month.

When I told the madam of the house I would be leaving, the woman became upset and vowed to make drastic changes in my responsibilities. My parents were not convinced by such promises, so they took me off the job.

On my last day at the job I was paid the $25, that I was due, by check. But somehow she must have managed to take the check out of my purse and neatly closed it back up. Before leaving for home, noting the partly closed purse, I complained about the missing check. We both looked for it, but it was never found. I went home with no money. My parents filed a complaint in the Small Claims Court, but the charges were dropped because she never appeared in court. I never received a dime for all that hard work.

Throughout my teenage years, I held similar jobs for the summer months when I was in New York. One summer, when I was 17 or 18, I took care of a little nine-year-old boy who lived with his mother in the heart of Manhattan. The boy's name was Michael and the two lived in a furnished suite in mid-Manhattan between 5th and 6th Avenues. I was sent there by the employment agency. My sole job was to serve as a parent and/or companion to Michael. All other chores, such as housework, washing, and shopping for food were done by someone else. However, my job felt very confining because Michael began to depend upon me for everything. His mother came home in the evenings when Michael was asleep, so he seldom saw her, although he spoke with her on the phone several times each day. This employer paid me every week, and very well. It was several years later that I learned what she did for a living. She was a call-girl and a madam who managed a very successful "escort" service.

After my second year of college, I had to withdraw to get on more solid footing financially. To earn enough money to pay off the accumulated college debt to Kittrell, and save enough to get me going at Delaware State College, I felt my best solution was to get a sleep-in job. That is when I went to work for Amy and Paul Barry in Forest Hills, New York. They had one child, a two-year-old named Judy. The pay was good and the responsibilities manageable. I worked there for one year and one summer before returning to college.

After graduation from college, I became quite involved in my professional career of education. The information listed next describes the extent of that involvement:

- Filing Clerk; Bureau of Internal Revenue, New York City, summer 1945.
- Vacation Bible School Program: Teacher and Supervisor under Directorship of Congressman Adam Clayton Powell, Jr., Abyssinian Baptist Church, New York City (Harlem), New York. Summers only.
- Matriculated, 1948, in the Master's Program, Teachers College, Columbia University. For the next five summers I attended school and graduated in 1952 with a master's degree in the Teaching of History and the Social Studies.
- Teacher: Social Studies and Citizenship Education, Civics Education – grades 7 and 8, Director of Drama Club and Debating Time for Juniors, Responsible for Annual Black Studies Program, Founder and Coach of Girls Basketball Team, Booker T. Washington, Jr. High School, Dover, Delaware, 1945-1957
- Teacher: United States History and The Social Studies – grades 11 and 12, William Henry Comprehensive High School, Dover, Delaware, 1957-1960.
- Teacher: World Economic Geography – 9th grade girls, Beth Jacob Junior High School, Williamsburg Jewish School System, New York City, New York, 1961.

- Teacher: Core Curriculum of English and Social Studies – Junior High School No. 5, grades 7 and 8, Trenton, New Jersey, 1962, 1964.
- Participating Teacher – Princeton University Summer Schools Institute, Summer 1965, Princeton, New Jersey.
- Teacher Education Demonstration – Trenton State College, Summer Seminar for Teachers Education Majors, Trenton State College, Trenton, New Jersey.
- Cooperating Teacher; Secondary Education Majors, Trenton State College, Trenton, New Jersey, 1965-1968.
- Rutgers, The State University, New Brunswick, New Jersey. Extension Division. Satisfactorily completed course – Urban Education (20 hours), 1967.
- Team Leader-Master Teacher; National Teachers Corp Project – Trenton Public School System and Trenton State College, Trenton, New Jersey, 1968-1970.
- Assistant Director: Career Opportunities Program – Trenton Public School System, 1971 for 14 months.

Notes on Undergraduate Courses I Taught

<u>Junior Professional Experience</u>

Conduct seminars in educational and teaching theory to secondary education juniors and supervise the practical implementation of this theory in a classroom setting where the cooperating teacher functions as the continuous on-base teacher educator. Maintain a teaching-learning posture and professional growth expectation with the cooperating teacher through conferences, regular visitations, and critiques that are continuous, to make sure the person has the maximum opportunity to learn and grow.

<u>Senior Student Teaching Supervision</u>

Supervise secondary education seniors in a variety of schools, where they have been placed to practice in a classroom setting with a cooperating teacher, full-time continuous implementation of the required competencies for effective teaching behaviors. With gradual immersion, the senior ultimately assumes the full teaching load of the cooperating teacher, not to exceed five classes per day, for a full semester in both junior (middle) and senior high school.

Secondary Education Senior Student Teaching Seminar

A culminating seminar designed to be taken concurrently with senior student teaching that will examine and analyze teaching behaviors and student teaching experiences in relation to specific competencies. Students are expected to examine theory in relation to practice with clinical professor and supervisor.

Graduate Courses I Taught

"Curriculum Construction or Design in the Urban Schools" required courses for all students seeking a master's degree in management or school administration.

Professional Titles held at the College:

- Assistant Professor, School of Education, Trenton State College, Trenton, New Jersey, 1971.
- Associate Professor, School of Education, Trenton State College, Trenton, New Jersey. Promoted to this rank in 1983.

Academic Responsibilities to the Graduate and Undergraduate Programs at Trenton State College:

- Instructor in Educational Theory.
- Supervisor of junior and senior secondary education majors.
- Instructor of the Competency Based Teacher Education Program for secondary education majors.
- Curriculum Specialist for paraprofessionals.
- Curriculum Specialist in Urban Education.
- Program Planning Specialist.
- Student Conference and Counseling Service Specialist.
- Curriculum Specialist in the theory and practice of curriculum construction and development.

Academic & Curriculum Involvement Beyond Trenton State College

Planned and coordinated a three-day workshop – "Personal Growth and Positive Self-Esteem" New Grange School for emotionally disturbed and perceptually impaired children, seniors, age 17-20 years. Located on grounds of Holy Angels Catholic School, South Broad Street, Trenton, New Jersey.

Member and Presenter on the Parker brothers' team – "Personal and Academic Growth and Development for Children and Educators." Founders; Dr. William Parker and Dr. Robert Parker. Other team members were Mr. Hugh Strayhorn and Dr. Elsie M. Collins. Workshops and presentations were conducted at schools, organizations, colleges, churches, etc.

Guest of 100 eighth graders at Smithfield-Selma Middle School, Smithfield, North Carolina. Concentration of our discussion was "Personal Goals and Values for Academic Success," April 25, 1988. Mr. Arnold – School Principal.

Other Academic and Community Involvement

1. Community and College Relations Committee (1984-1987)
2. Admissions Committee (1983-1986)
3. Affirmative Action Committee (1984-1987)
4. New Jersey Education Association including (NEA, MEA, and Faculty Association) since coming to State of New Jersey.
5. Phi Delta Kappa – (Rider College Campus) Membership since 1979
6. Academic Affairs Council – 1988-1989
7. Faculty Senate (re-elected Spring 1988) for fourth three-year term.
8. Promotions Committee, 1987-88 and 1988-89.
9. Academic Affairs Committee, 1986-87, 1987-88.
10. Minority Executive Committee (continuous membership since 1979)

11. Inducted into the American Association of Doctorates (New York University), 1977.

Professional growth from 1985 through 1988

a) Sabbatical Leave, Spring 1988, second semester. Researching material and traveling in the south, principally in North Carolina in a continuous posture for the publication of a book entitled Small-Town Strutters, a biographical sketch of selected families in a small southern village. January through June 1988.
b) Recipient of Presidential Citation in recognition of exemplary experiences that honor my Alma Mater, Delaware State College in Dover, Delaware, by the National Association for Equal Opportunity in Higher Education (NAFEO) at the Hilton Hotel, Washington, D.C., April 11, 1987.
c) A 5-Day Research and Travel Experience in Goulds, Florida. I was the organizer and coordinator of the "Family and Friends Reunion Research Team." In addition, I was guest of the Principal at the Mays Middle School in Gould where I responded to and participated in a discussion on "Teaching Competencies and Teacher Behaviors" with the principal and other school administrators. April 1985.
d) Community Educational Advisory Council (CEAC). Function as a parent advocate (part-time) to help locate and articulate school policy to effect parents and advise them of available options in the interest of their children. Spring 1985-present. (Founder)
e) Concerned Parents Organization of Hamilton School District. Was an organization of white parents, mostly, who asked to merge with CEAC.

I represented the School of Education, The College of New Jersey (formerly Trenton State College), at the National Association for Equal Opportunity in Higher Education (NAFEO) at a four-day conference, Washington, D.C. I served as a participant in the question/answer/discussion sessions. Also purchased, for the School of Education, pertinent and relevant materials (tapes, pamphlets, books, etc.) and made them available to colleagues. Served in this capacity beginning in 1983.

Publications (Books, Paper, Film, etc.)

- Leinwand, Gerald, and Collins, Elsie M.: Poverty and the Poor: Problems of American Society Series, New York: Washington Square Press, Inc., 1968.
- Leinwand, Gerald; Munce, Bernice; Collins, Elsie M.: The Negro in the City, and Civil Rights and Civil Liberties, Problems of American Society Series, Washington Square Press, Inc., 1969.
- Collins, Elsie M., Capuzzi, Frank (Collaborator) "Tomorrow's Teachers Today," (a film for television) Bhaduda Film Associates, Pittsburgh, Pennsylvania, 1975.
  My Doctoral Internship Certification: with a grant of $8,000 from the New Jersey Education Association, we were asked to make a film for television that is expressive of teacher education and the training of teachers at Trenton State College.
- Collins, Elsie M., Who Am I? Proud, Black, and God's Child: I Am Somebody: Prepared for distribution by Educational Testing Service, Princeton, New Jersey, 1978.
  This is the only authentic historical account of the Black families who populated the township of Wilson's Mills, Johnston County, North Carolina, as early as 1800. This booklet of 55 pages is on display in the Johnston Division of the Public Library, Smithfield, North Carolina since 1980 and the Heritage Center, Market Street, Smithfield, North Carolina.
- Collins, Elsie M., *Smalltown Strutters*, (Editors: Paul R. Shelly & Elsie M. Collins), Trenton, New Jersey, 1996.
- Collins, Elsie M., *Gentle People From a Not-So-Gentle Past*, (Editors: Paul R. Shelly & Elsie M. Collins), Trenton, New Jersey, 2002.

Membership in Organizations, Societies, Etc.

- Community Educational Advisory Council, Organizer and Chairperson, Hamilton Township, New Jersey.
- Alpha Kappa Alpha Sorority
- Phil Delta Kappa, Research – Service – Leadership
- Trenton Branch, NAACP

- Trenton Branch, Urban League
- Christian Children's Fund, Inc. – I am a continuous contributor to the Christian Children's Fund since 1983. Have helped educate several children in Africa.
- National Alliance of Black Educators
- National Council of the Social Studies
- SAVE our Children Community Organization
- National Education Association
- Mercer County Education Association
- New Jersey Association of College Faculties
- American Teacher Association
- National Association of Christians and Jews
- St. Paul United Methodist Church: Choir member/soloist, Administrative Board, Council on Ministries, Chairperson of Missions
- Laity Representative to Ministry Council for Southern Conference of United Methodist Church of Trenton Ecumenical Area Ministry (TEAM)
- Association for Supervision and Curriculum Development
- United Negro College Fund
- Southern Poverty Law Center
- Board Consultant for Board of Directors, South Olden Apartments, Inc.
- President, Board of Directors, East Trenton Day Care Council
- Secretary, Board of Directors, East Trenton Center
- Vice President, Board of Directors, Rescue Mission of Greater Trenton (integrated this board as first female and first minority member in 1980).
- Trustee/Board of Directors, John O. Wilson Neighborhood Service Center, Hamilton Township, Trenton, New Jersey
- Board of Directors, Urban Mission Alliance
- Special Assignment, State Department of Education, Trenton, New Jersey, 1982
- Evaluating Team for Secondary Schools of the State of New Jersey

My assignment dealt with curriculum, instruction and instructors at Trenton Central High School, Trenton, New Jersey.

- Board of Directors, Young Scholars Institute
- Board of Commissioners, The Heritage Center, Smithfield, North Carolina.

Addresses and Speeches Delivered

"Education, A Must for Progress," Commencement Address – Johnston County Central High School, Smithfield, North Carolina. May, 1957.

"Characteristics of an Outstanding Educator" - Short Journey Elementary School, Smithfield, North Carolina. May, 1967 Honoring the Graduates of Short Journey Elementary School Occasion: A Special Tribute to the Retiring Second Grade Teacher, and Cousin Ione Vinson, after 47 years of continuous successful service in education.

"Teacher Preparation and School Integration" 65th Annual Founders Day Celebration. Epsilon Iota Omega and Delta Lambda Chapters. Alpha Kappa Alpha Sorority. Delaware State College, Dover, Delaware. Sunday, February 18, 1973.

"Parents Take a Look at Thorough and Efficient Education – A State Mandate." Paraprofessionals of School District No. 13. Newark, New Jersey. February, 1974.

"Breaking Out of the Fish Bowl and Going to Junior High." Sixth Grade Graduating Class. Woodrow Wilson Elementary School. Trenton, New Jersey. June, 1976.

"The Little Eagle Who Thought He Was A Chicken." Sixth Grade Graduating Class. Monument Elementary School. Trenton, New Jersey. June, 1977.

"I Am God's Child: Black, Beautiful and Proud." Homecoming Celebration of the Sons and Daughters of Wilson's Mills. Union Hill A.M.E. Church. Wilson's Mills, North Carolina. October 15, 1978.

"Are You Bored With Life? Occasion: Recipient of the Community Service Award. Presented by the Teacher Organization, Excellence

Through Education (ETE). Scholarship Dinner. Hamilton Township, Trenton, New Jersey. April 22, 1979.

"Thanks, Mom and Dad, For Caring." East Trenton Day Care Council. Promotion and Graduation Day. Trenton, New Jersey. August, 1979.

"We Called Her Sis Sallie." Occasion: The Sallie A. Richardson Missionary Area Society. Banquet, The naming of the Society after my Aunt Sallie. North Carolina Conference Central District A.M.E. Church. Cooper Junior High School. Clayton, North Carolina. April 29 1979.

"Christian Women On the Move – Yesterday and Today." The Thirteenth Annual Women's Day Service. The Church on the Hill A.M.E. Zion Church. New York City, New York. November 18, 1979.

"Making It On Scraps." Mother's Day Speaker. St. Paul United Methodist Church (an integrated church). Trenton, New Jersey. May 11, 1980.

"Why I Like School So Much." Sixth grade graduating class. Caldwalder Elementary School. Trenton, New Jersey. June, 1980.

"New Directions, Accountability, Responsibility" (Boule' Theme) Thirty-fifth Annual Boule', Chi Eta Phi Sorority. International Organization of Registered Nurses of the United States and Africa. Hotel Roosevelt, New York City, New York. June 25, 1980.

"The Black Female" (a position paper). Theme: "Understanding the Impact of Cultural Diversity in the World of Work." Bell Labs, Holmdel, New Jersey. April, 1981.

"The Triangle That Shapes the American Lifestyle." The 58th Annual Parents' Day Celebration. Delaware State College, Dover, Delaware. October, 1982.

"Benevolence Is The Art of Caring." Fourteenth Annual Luncheon. Benevolent Club '75. Sharaton Centre, New York City, New York. June, 1983.

"Christian Women Must Meet Today's Challenges." St. Paul A.M.E. Zion Church. Trenton, New Jersey. September 14, 1984.

"This Is The House By The Side of The Road." A Homecoming-Family Reunion. Miami, Florida. April, 1985.

"Christian Women, This is Charity!" Women's Day Celebration. Shiloh Baptist Church. Bordentown, New Jersey. October 26, 1986.

"Reminiscing Fifty Plus Years Ago When We Were in High School." Afternoon speaker. Johnston Central High School Alumni Association Conference. May, 2002.

"The Love of a Christian Woman," Women's Day Speaker, Millers Chapel A.M.E. Zion Church. Goldsboro, North Carolina. May 2003.

Integrating St. Paul United Methodist Church

St. Paul Methodist Episcopal Church was a "white" church back in 1964. The only individuals who worshipped at that church were Caucasian. African Americans who were Methodist worshippers attended a Methodist Church located on Fountain Street in Trenton. The name of the church was Asbury Methodist Episcopal Church. There were several Methodist churches in Trenton, but the nearest one to my home on Spring Street was St. Paul, located on West State Street.

With two very young children and no car, I had already checked out the situation and studied the distance from my house to the church. I was sure I could walk this distance each Sunday morning with my children. I would push baby Kimberly, who was eleven months old, in the stroller. Leslie, three and a few months, could walk beside me. The distance wasn't too great, and if we took our time, little Leslie would not get too tired.

One Sunday morning in July 1964, I woke up early and got all of us prepared for our first visit to St. Paul Methodist Episcopal Church. We left home early enough and arrived at the church at an acceptable time.

Judging from the order of the service, church had just begun, for parishioners were still arriving. A few people had just entered the church prior to our entrance, so I knew it was at an acceptable time.

In the church vestibule, I adjusted the children. I took Kimberly out of the stroller and stood her on the floor and placed the stroller in a corner. I then took the baby by the hand, while Leslie stood quietly beside me. I gently pushed the door to the sanctuary open, and had one of the biggest surprises of my life. There was a sea of white folks, probably 300. I closed the door immediately and stood frozen in my tracks. But, we had been seen. About five individuals came out to the vestibule to meet us, and ask what I wanted. I didn't know any of the people who came to talk to me. However, I was invited to come into the sanctuary and worship with them. And so we did.

The news that a black woman was sitting in the audience worshipping with an all-white audience spread throughout the sanctuary. I was aware of a disturbance in the congregation that my presence had caused, and I, too, was uneasy.

St. Paul's congregation was accustomed to the presence of black people in their church. Their organist was black. His name was David Carroll, a graduate of Fisk University in Tennessee and University of Chicago. Mr. Carroll was also a former Professor of Music at Virginia State College before moving to Trenton with his wife Marie, an accomplished pianist. But these individuals were hired to perform a service; they were not members of St. Paul.

Into the following week, I received several phone calls from a few members of the church encouraging me to return to the church. Among these individuals were Jack and Jean Wilson of Morrisville, Pennsylvania and Wilbur Johnson, who was the music teacher and chorus director at Junior High School No. 5, where I taught.

Thus encouraged, I did return, and immediately became a very active member of the church. Jack Wilson and his wife had three children of their own at that time. Jack volunteered to pick up three-year-old Leslie each Sunday morning and bring her to Sunday school with his children. I would walk to church later with Kimberly.

Over the next several years, as I continued to attend St. Paul, I became more and more involved in the church activities, and so did my two little girls. Leslie and Kimberly became quite popular and made many church friends.

But the presence of a non-white family at St. Paul upset many of the members of this all-white congregation. Fortunately, the pastors who served St. Paul, by and large, were not prone to treat our family differently and gave us due respect.

Those members who could not deal with a racially diverse congregation left St. Paul and joined Methodist churches elsewhere. They exercised their right to flee to the church of their choice, perhaps afraid of a black "takeover" of some sort, or they simply held a racist attitude. Most of them joined Trinity Methodist Church, which was located on Pennington Road, near Trenton State College. During the first year of church integration, I estimate that about 25-30% of the congregation left St. Paul. Although the rate of withdrawal from the church slowed down somewhat, it still continued over a period of several years.

Following a few years of church involvement, I officially joined St. Paul's and so did David and Marie Carroll. Both Leslie and Kimberly joined with other children at the appropriate age. Eventually, other African Americans joined the church as it became known as a place where they would be respectfully treated, if not welcomed.

Over the several years of my membership at St. Paul, I feel that I became a major contributor to the spiritual life, growth and development of St. Paul. Some of my roles involved:

- Helping write a proposal to create St. Paul's Latch Key After School Program and serving as a board member of that program;
- Co-directing, with Elizabeth Campell, youth activities;
- Chair of Missions Committee of St. Paul;
- Singing and soloing with the Chancel Choir;
- Serving as the church's representative to TEAM (Trenton Ecumenical Area Ministry);
- Serving as the church's representative on the Ecumenical West Ward;
- Coordinating Vacation Bible School;
- Teaching Young Adult Sunday School;
- Participating on Administrative Council

Some forty years after joining, I remained a member of St. Paul's Church, which recently merged with Trenton's First United Methodist Church and is now called Turning Point United Methodist Church.

Nana and How She Was Taken from the Family

She was affectionately called Nana by just about everyone who knew her. Professionally, she was a concert artist, pianist, recitalist, and a very busy person doing church work as the wife of the minister in the United Methodist Church.

When my husband Douglas and I were going through difficult times in our marriage, Nana was a stabilizer. She counseled me, encouraged me and held my hands. We visited each other daily and gave comfort when needed. After Douglas and I sold our home in Camden in 1964 and I moved myself and the children to Trenton, I kept in very close contact with Nana. I was supervising her medical program and her living conditions in general. In the 1990s, when Nana was in her mid-eighties, her home had become a problem to maintain. I convinced her to give up the house and move into a senior citizen housing complex. She agreed. Several of us, including my close friends Amy and Joe, helped move Nana to a government-regulated senior citizen housing unit on Mickle Boulevard in Camden. She was very happy there in her efficiency apartment.

Nana had supervised the selection of furniture, precious items, dishes and other valuable items she wished to bring to her new apartment. Reilly Cruse (a friend), Taylor Collins (Doug's cousin), my daughters and I, plus my friends Amy and Joe, stayed in close contact with Nana to make sure she was securely settled in her apartment and living a normal life.

The building was federally funded and supervised for the convenience of senior citizens. Therefore, Nana's two small incomes supplied her with enough income for her to be quite comfortable. Then in her mid-eighties, she managed some of her affairs, did her shopping, drove her car (Doug's cousin Taylor made sure it was in good running condition) around town, and prepared her own meals. Meals-on-Wheels brought her lunch each day.

I supervised her medical program. I drove down to Camden and took Nana to the doctor whenever it was requested by the doctor. I also supervised her checking and savings accounts, and made sure all major bills were paid. I carried on telephone conversations with Nana weekly, and visited her small apartment twice a month, usually Saturday, unless there was a special need to visit more often. There were some situations that made it necessary for me to take Nana home with me for a few days. One of these situations was following emergency surgery for her esophagus. Nana spent almost a month with me and the girls. The other two stays at my home were recommended by Nana's doctor when he was monitoring her heart with a change of medication. I returned Nana to her home in Camden when the doctor suggested.

Because of Nana's physical condition, in particular a heart murmur, I thought it a good idea to have Nana register on the waiting list at the Methodist Home in Collingswood, New Jersey. This would guarantee her a small apartment at the facility whenever she wished to move in. This opportunity was not an open privilege for everyone, but had to be granted by a special board, otherwise a wait of twelve years was required before one was eligible to move into living quarters there immediately. I spoke to David Fluck about this possibility for Nana. Dr. Fluck, being a member of the Home's board, and in an influential position, made a number of phone calls. As a result, Nana was granted the opportunity to get on the waiting list with the privilege of moving in immediately. This process took about five months.

I was very excited about this privilege. I talked it over again with Nana, and made it clear that she needed to register and sign the document as soon as possible.

I went to Camden, picked up Nana and we both visited the Collingswood Manor Methodist Home. We ate brunch under the supervision of the director, read the documents, asked questions and filled in the required information. Nana refused to sign the documents. She stated that she was not ready to do so then, so we went home. It became clear to me that Nana did not intend to sign those papers, so I stopped asking, practically begging, her to do so.

However, Nana did sign some papers that later brought a great deal of unhappiness to her life.

The house where Nana lived, on Park Boulevard in Camden, belonged to Mary and Howard Stevenson of Dover, Delaware. It did not belong to Nana, as so many people believed. The couple later sold the house, but, with the advice of a reputable law firm in Camden, were told to give Nana $3,000 for her services and care of the property. These funds were to reimburse Nana for upkeep of the property, including minor repairs, payment of utilities, and general maintenance of the house. The Stevensons objected to such a payment, but offered $2,000 to Nana and she accepted it. All this was arranged and supervised by me on Nana's behalf. She then had to move to an apartment.

Subsequently, I contacted the Department of Welfare and the Department of Human and Social Services and asked for daily supervision for Nana. Together, we arranged for an individual to visit Nana four days per week for half a day. This individual would wash for her, prepare a meal and straighten up the apartment. I explained this idea to Nana, who rejected it immediately. I had time to convince Nana of the idea, since it would take a few months before it would be implemented. Slowly and carefully, I began to explain the advantages of this idea and other family members were also involved.

Meanwhile, a group of people from a nearby United Methodist Church, headed by self-appointed leaders, was also working on plans for Nana. Nana was encouraged by this group to sign a paper giving one of them Power-of-Attorney over her affairs. I had cautioned Nana on several occasions about signing papers given to her by friends. I encouraged her to contact me to explain a particular document's meaning to her. But Nana failed to contact me in this instance, so they were awarded Nana's Power-of-Attorney.

One Saturday I found, upon my arrival, that this group had moved Nana to a senior citizen complex somewhere in Camden.

I was stunned, speechless. After inquiring at the desk of the senior citizens complex where she had been living, without receiving any cooperation, I threatened to call the police if someone did not tell me the whereabouts of my mother-in-law. Reluctantly, a phone number and address for a nursing home were given to me. I immediately contacted the nursing home by phone, and made a visit. The administrators at the facility were very cooperative, but were bound by law to follow the instructions of the individual who had brought Nana there. Nana was unhappy and very surprised to find herself in a nursing home. She was shaking with anxiety, and asked me to please take her home. I explained to her again about the paper she had signed, which gave these people control over her affairs. But I promised I would do what I could for her.

For $500, I retained a lawyer immediately to launch an investigation and revoke the Power-of-Attorney agreement Nana had with this group. I later learned that this group and my attorney were political allies in the Camden government. I suspect I did not receive the best counseling and legal representation available. The lawyer suggested that the best way to get control of Nana's affairs was to go to court and declare her incompetent, and then ask the judge to appoint me as legal guardian. He told me that such a procedure would be costly, $5,000 to start, and that there was no guarantee the judge would make the requested assignment since I was not Nana's biological daughter. He further stated that I had no right to declare Nana incompetent because she was not incompetent, and she was not my mother. It saddened me to lose this battle to gain control of Nana's affairs.

Nana's physical condition began to deteriorate. After a few months, Nana was transferred to the fifth floor of the nursing facility at Collingswood Manor. At this point, she was unable to care for herself. Family members, friends and I continued to visit Nana as often as possible, and at each visit, Nana wanted me to take her back home to her apartment in Camden, New Jersey. Several of us took turns to drive down to Collingswood to visit Nana. The family continued to talk to the caregivers at the nursing home about her condition but we were prohibited from making any changes.

During Nana's confinement, her apartment was stripped and everything she had was taken by this church group and others. Nana's family was never contacted regarding the dismantling of her home, nor were any of her personal belongings ever seen. In Nana's home were many valuable family possessions. She had a valuable doll collection, that included dolls she played with as a child. She had her mother's dishes, silver, and glassware. She had her husband's degrees, awards, and library. She had her own musical collection, silverware and a complete communion silver service, to name a few. The church group took all of these possessions that belonged to the Collins' family.

I began to have health problems of my own, which resulted in major surgery in the fall of 2000. My medical treatment program was transferred to Woodbridge, Virginia, where my daughter Kimberly lived with her family.

I was busy undergoing special treatment and recuperating in Woodbridge, when I learned in February 2003 that Nana had passed away the previous Christmas. Charlotte Burns, Nana's granddaughter who lived in Seattle, Washington, was the only family member notified. Charlotte was Nana's only listed surviving family member. Since no other family members were notified and Charlotte did not attend the funeral, family members were absent from the funeral.

The Influence of David Fluck, MD

Pathologist, Helene Fuld Hospital;
Medical Examiner, State of New Jersey

As I matured into middle age, I continued to think of myself as an attractive woman. Perhaps I was not beautiful as some Americans still define it, based on Northern European features and skin color. Still, from what I could gather, my impact when I was dressed "to a tee," was stunning. My dress size was a perfect eight to ten, and I wore a nine narrow shoe. My height of 5'2" was well proportioned and fit perfectly in a weight package of 115 pounds. My skin was an even, dark brown color and my shoulder-length black hair framed me nicely. Indeed, I was referred to across the college campus at The College of New Jersey as the professor who knew the latest, classy fashions, and wore them well.

I was quite popular among men, white and black. But as a single parent with two young daughters, I chose on the side of a carefully controlled social life. I wanted to make sure that the images my daughters had of their mother was exemplary. In fact, I completely cut out dating during the children's formative years. I only began dating occasionally when they had become teenagers. By the time Dr. David Fluck, a leading physician in the Mercer County area, who happened to be white (of German descent), and I became good friends, both daughters were away attending college. Dr. Fluck was twelve years my senior.

Dr. Fluck's wife, Kaye, had died in 1978 and I, like many other members of St. Paul United Methodist Church, attended her wake and funeral. Following these services, I met the family members and expressed my sympathy to them.

About one year following these services, I received a phone call from Dr. Fluck, who engaged me in small talk and general conversation. He also invited me to have dinner with him at his home at my convenience. I graciously accepted this invitation. However, following church on the very next Sunday, Dr. Fluck had prepared a special dinner for me at his home. This was the beginning of a special friendship between the two of us that lasted for the next six years.

Our Relationship Blossoms. Our special relationship became common knowledge among members of St. Paul's Church. Dr. Fluck was openly involved with me. In his "take charge" manner, we sat together in church if we were not involved in separate programs, such as my singing in the choir or his presiding over a program. Since we came to church in separate cars, because each came from his own home, I would follow him in my car as he drove to his home after church services. We spent a great many Sunday afternoons together. Often we went out to eat, and sometimes he prepared dinner and we ate at his home. I was still teaching at the college, so I had homework to do. Often I would bring it with me and did my school work preparation right there in his living room, while he continued to prepare the food and do other chores.

One of Dave's favorite pastime events for Sunday afternoon was to go sightseeing in Pennsylvania. He grew up in Pennsylvania and knew quite a bit about Bucks County, as well as the Pennsylvania Dutch (German) Country. He enjoyed telling me about these areas. He also loved to visit museums, botanical gardens and art galleries in Philadelphia and New York City. We occasionally went to Princeton University to visit the cathedral on campus and attend church services there.

When we went out to eat on Sunday afternoon, it was always at a top-notch restaurant. Dave made it his business to introduce himself and his date in this manner, "This is Dr. Elsie M. Collins, and I am Dr. David Fluck." I was always given "top drawer," white glove treatment. This meant, also, that my conduct had to match this treatment and my appearance as well. I was quite aware of these requirements and to my knowledge, I always rose to the occasion.

Dr. Fluck was quite protective of me, and would not accept insults of any kind from anyone. I recall an incident where Dr. Fluck needed to take a stand, and he did.

The restaurant that Dr. Fluck took me to that Sunday evening was in Pennsylvania. I was dressed in a two-piece black Persian lamb suit with a white silk blouse. My Geri-curled hair was cut in a boyish bob with a point at the base of the neck. I recall that the restaurant was a mansion that had been converted into an exclusive restaurant where individuals could enjoy a delicious meal in an elegant atmosphere. Each group of tables, spaced generously apart, had two waitresses who stood in assigned areas. These waitresses, very specially dressed, had different assignments; one was responsible for food only and the other was responsible for alcoholic drinks only. Dr. Fluck and I were seated by the Maitre D'.

After we were seated, the food waitress was to take over. She did not, but stood in place as if she did not see the people at her table. Dr. Fluck and I exchanged small talk as we waited to give our order. After what I thought was a long wait, Dr. Fluck became agitated and loudly called to a waitress for service. But instead of asking for service, he requested the presence of the supervisor. The waitress began to apologize, but Dr. Fluck was not interested and demanded an audience with the supervisor. Dr. Fluck explained to the supervisor what the problem was and gave his personal interpretation of what he observed. The supervisor was apologetic and fired the waitress effective immediately. David and I enjoyed a wonderful evening at dinner in this elegant atmosphere.

David constantly encouraged me and urged me to center stage where my capabilities could be seen and appreciated. His membership on the Board of Directors of the East Trenton Community Center and the East Trenton Day Care Center also meant that I should have membership on these boards. This was arranged and I soon joined the Board of Directors of both centers and eventually became President of each board, as well. David was also sponsor and president of the organization called, "The Last Monday Tea." This was an organization of senior citizens living in Greater Trenton who met on the last Monday of each month for fun, lunch and a short program. I was encouraged to attend these meetings and be responsible for the music and possibly some type of games, if needed. So I assisted David in carrying out the program.

As our friendship blossomed and deepened, there were many honest soul-searching conversations about our relationship and feelings for one another. At times, this learned man was shy and hesitant and he looked to me to lead in certain aspects of the relationship.

David's children grew to accept and respect me. There were three of them, and they had moved away from Trenton many years ago. All were married and had children, with the exception of his son, George, who lived with his wife Lenore in Central New Jersey. His younger daughter, Sarah, lived with her family in Maryland near the Chesapeake Bay. Dr. Fluck's oldest daughter lives in Bangor, Maine with her family. His oldest daughter, Charlotte, and I occasionally communicated with each other via mail. And when she visited her father, the three of us went out and had a great deal of fun.

The Promotions Committee. My friendship and association with Dr. Fluck was pretty well known throughout the Greater Trenton area. Occasionally, he would show up at meetings, programs, conferences, and/or boards if I were involved and quietly take a seat in the rear of the room. Because of his public stature as pathologist and medical examiner, he would often be introduced or called on to make remarks if he was noticed in the crowd.

It was a first when a citizen not connected with The College of New Jersey (then Trenton State College) made a request to appear before the Promotions Committee and speak on behalf of an individual. Dr. Fluck made such a request, on my behalf, and was granted permission. His request to appear before the Promotions Committee made great campus news and even appeared in the campus newsletter.

Whether or not his presentation made a difference in the decisions of the Promotions Committee I can't be certain, but after the meeting I did receive my promotion from Assistant Professor to the senior level of Associate Professor.

And Neither Will Elsie Attend. As President of the Community Educational Advisory Committee (CEAC), and with other members, I was involved in correcting a problem concerning curriculum and entertainment at Grice Middle School in Hamilton, New Jersey. The school district's top officials were impatient with me and the CEAC organization and were determined to lay down the law with me. These top school officials were as follows: the Superintendent of Schools, the Assistant Superintendent in Charge of Staff Development; the School Principal, plus the teacher who was in charge of the program. The Superintendent announced that the top school officials would confer with me alone in the Principal's office and all other members should go home.

David Fluck got involved when I explained to him my concerns that I was being isolated. He registered his objections with the school officials, stating that there would be no meeting with Elsie unless he was in attendance. When the school officials objected, Dr. Fluck replied that he would be in contact with friends at Princeton University who would be very happy to set up an extensive interview with the Sixty Minutes television crew on the topic of problems in the Hamilton Township School System. Tempers calmed and attitudes changed. Dr. Fluck and I met in conference with the top school officials of Hamilton and rationally discussed the need for change in the school curriculum.

The Literary Club. Membership in the Trenton area Literary Club was very selective. Of the twenty-five members, only eight or nine were women, with the vast majority being men. All where white.

It became clear that membership in this club was very carefully thought out. Judging from the academic accomplishments of the membership, the club made a deliberate statement regarding class quality. Examples of credentials of membership were as follows: superintendent of schools, medical doctors, and doctors of philosophy, college professors, lawyers, judges and ministers. The women were also accomplished. Some were wives of accomplished husbands, accomplished individuals themselves, or both. The members were all white-Anglo Saxon Protestants.

The club met every month. A member or a group of members volunteered to entertain at each meeting. They also selected the next meeting place and sent out invitations to the members.

During the many years when Dave and I were special friends, Dave entertained the Literary Group at his home several times. I knew my role as the hostess, and made it my business to greet the membership graciously on each occasion.

Our relationship was out of the ordinary in America. This unique friendship raised many an eyebrow, but was also smiled upon by most of our friends and acquaintances.

Dave was protective of our friendship and would, at no time, allow me to be insulted. He knew what to say when necessary, and just how to say it and did not hesitate to do so. Therefore, I knew all about the Literary Club; and its membership knew all about me.

There was a surprise for me on one particular occasion when Dave was the host. As the guests began to arrive five to ten minutes prior to the meeting, I assumed my role as hostess, greeting the guests, showing them where to hang their coats, and inviting them to the living room where the meeting was to be held.

Refreshments for the occasion were already prepared. Some portions of the refreshments were catered, and the rest was done by Dave and me. The dining room table and chairs were arranged to accommodate the guests when it was time to serve refreshments. The living room furniture, which included borrowed chairs, was arranged in semi-circles to give the guests the ability to almost always face each other as they communicated and discussed literary issues.

When all the expected members had gathered, the meeting proceeded. After the initial business had been conducted, the president of the Literary Group called to me and asked if I would like to join the group when they began to discuss this month's book. I was stunned. I hesitated for a moment as I considered the request and then declined gracefully, thanking the club's president for his generosity.

I have always considered myself a standard bearer for my race and I knew I had a responsibility to promote and uphold its dignity, and I saw it as my mission. The odds seemed against me at this time, but I knew if I believed I would fail, failure would be certain. What I did not know about the context of this meeting greatly outweighed what I knew. I knew if I tried to participate with no academic foundation to support me, I could bring embarrassment to myself and to my race. Following my better judgment, I declined.

Cream of the Crop. An upscale dress-down affair is the ball sponsored by the Northeastern Regional Links Annual Affair. Even though it is an invitational affair, expensive tickets had to be purchased for admittance to the ball. As usual, I received an invitation. That year, I decided I would attend, but I had to convince Dr. Fluck just how important it was for us to attend together. So I carefully chose the day I would discuss it with him, as well as the period of time when the discussion would take place. My strategy paid off, for he agreed to attend.

At this gala affair, there would be at least five or six African American doctors in attendance from Trenton whom he knew, as well as his very good friend and personal physician Dr. John Marshall. Doctors in attendance would include: Dr. Fraser, Dr. Williams, Dr. Thompson, Dr. Hayling, and Dr. Sullivan. Other doctors from the northeastern region of the Links who lived in the State of New York, Pennsylvania, Delaware and Maryland, as well as New Jersey, would also be in attendance. Dr. Fluck would certainly know many of them, as well.

I secured our tickets from one of my college colleagues, Dr. Helene McRae, President of the Trenton Chapter of Links.

The festivities were well underway when we arrived. After Dave checked our wraps, we entered the dance floor. Dave was greeted immediately by his friend, John Marshall, and ushered to John's table where we met other guests. Following introductions and etc., Dave and I danced and chatted quietly. Dave soon became one of the "good old boys," as his friends and colleagues greeted and welcomed him. I was not at all a stranger among the Links, for Mrs. Bernice Munce, my mentor and others were working hard to bring me into the organization. Dave laughed and chatted with his friends, drank a cocktail or two, and danced, mostly with me.

Dave and I left the ball early. As a matter of fact, I had promised him that I would not be unhappy if we left the ball before it was over. As we traveled home from the ball, we chatted about the quality of the affair, the people, decorations, hors d'oevres, and music. I knew that Dave really did enjoy himself as he chuckled about being the only white man present.

David had a very dear friend who was a professor at a medical school in California. The friend was ill. Dave flew to California to visit this friend twice during his relationship with me. On his last trip to visit his friend, he was saddened by his friends' physical deterioration, afraid he would not live much longer. The friend died a few months after that visit.

The next summer the wife of his deceased friend insisted upon coming east and spending some time visiting David. She said she was attracted to David and wished to cultivate a relationship. David told me about her request, and said he was trying to discourage her from coming. He also told her that he had a special friend in Trenton, and there could be no relationship between the two of them. The lady came anyway and made herself a guest at David's house. She soon discovered that David indeed had a very special friend, and her name was Elsie. The friend returned to California without accomplishing her personal goal.

Dr. Fluck was a sensitive man who was well aware of the struggles of the oppressed. He took advantage of opportunities to address situations of oppression and discrimination in the Lawrence-Trenton area where he lived. Often we would engage in in-depth discussion about the social and economic climate in America. He did not like Dr. Martin Luther King's method of getting his message out to the greater population. He criticized King for organizing marches and saw them as being disruptive and alienating southern whites. "King should have found other methods of getting his message across," he often stated.

David also expressed his dissatisfaction with the lack of presence of African Americans in white collar jobs in downtown Trenton. At first he felt that they did not apply for these jobs and wondered why. I helped him understand that the practice of job discrimination was the problem. African Americans were qualified, but not hired.

David joined several other doctors, the medical crew and a variety of building contractors to build a hospital in the Congo (now Zaire), in Africa. David stayed involved in this project. When the hospital was completed, David became part of an international medical team to staff the hospital. Teams and/or individuals were required to spend at least a block of two years each time. David spent two blocks of time in the Congo, which totaled a period of four years of voluntary medical service in that country.

Reading was one of David's principal hobbies and buying books was part of that hobby. His home was filled with thousands of books, which were stored in one of the three bedrooms, as well as the entire basement of his home. David knew the content of most of his books. He would get involved in a subject area and make reference to a particular book, as well as a particular writer. I noted that among the many magazines he subscribed to, none of them were about African Americans. I asked him about this lack and his excuse was flimsy. I decided to bring copies of Ebony magazine to his home and mixed them among the other magazines he was receiving.

Dave loved to travel and every year left New Jersey and traveled afar. Being twelve years his junior, I was still working, and therefore, unable to travel with him. Sometimes he drove to visit his daughter in Bangor, Maine or to Chesapeake, Virginia to visit the other daughter. But then there were trips he took out of the country such as Hong Kong, England, Australia, and New Zealand. When he returned from these trips, he always brought me enchanting gifts.

One evening in the mid 1980's, George Fluck, his son, called me about five o'clock in the early evening. I knew from the tone of his voice and its urgency that there was concern. He told me that his father had suffered a stroke earlier that day and had been taken to Mercer Medical Center. He was in the care of his physician, Dr. John Marshall, who was on staff there. He told me that he had tried to reach me earlier, but was told that I was out in the field visiting students. I was given the number to his phone in his private room, but was told he should receive no visitors that evening.

I called and spoke with him as soon as I was allowed to do so. He assured me that he would be all right in a few days. He would speak with Dr. John Marshall later and get a clearer picture of what the problem was. Dave remained in the hospital for a few days and then was moved to the Rehabilitation Center in Lawrenceville, New Jersey. There he received therapy necessary to aid him in walking.

I went to see him every day. My best time was during my lunch, and just before I went supervising students who were a distance from the college.

Sue Enters the Picture. Dr. Fluck's medical training was done at the Hahneman Hospital and the University of Pennsylvania in Philadelphia, Pennsylvania. Also connected to the University hospital was a nursing unit. This was an era where students who wished to become nurses matriculated for training. It was here that he met his first wife, Kaye. As he explained to me, he and Kaye liked each other immediately, and soon became very good friends. There was another young lady at the school who also liked him, and her name was Sue. At times, though, Sue became a bit aggressive and demanding. He finally had to tell Sue that Kaye was his steady girl and he was making plans to marry her. Sue eventually married another man and Dave married Kaye.

Over the years, Sue became a widow. In the late 1970's, after David became a widower and I became his regular companion, Sue kept in contact with David.

During David's stay at the Rehabilitation Center, however, Sue became his constant companion. Initially, I was grateful for her attentiveness to his needs and deep concern. She spent days and many evenings with him carrying out the doctors' orders for rehabilitation. When Dave was released from the Center and sent home, she went home with him to continue the therapy. Within a year after returning home, their engagement was announced.

... and I step back. I was aware of David's changing situation, including Sue's continued presence. When I observed first hand Sue's "take complete charge" manner, I thought it best to take a step back and perhaps take myself out of the picture entirely. I would continue to call David occasionally to see how he was doing, but would curtail other contact with him.

Dr. John Marshall, Dave's personal physician as well as his confidant, called me to chat and to advise me. He wanted to know why I gave up on Dave, instead of fighting for him. He advised me to "go for it." I promised Dr. Marshall I would think it through and get back to him with my decision. After a week of soul searching, and weighing the pros and cons, I contacted Dr. Marshall with my decision. It was a no. I decided to withdraw completely and have virtually no further personal contact with Dr. Fluck. Dr. Marshall was disappointed and told me so.

David and Sue married at her church, St. Mark's United Methodist Church, in Hamilton Square, New Jersey. Many friends of the couple attended the marriage. I had no invitation, but attended the marriage ceremony. The couple moved into Dave's home in Lawrence to live.

Sue was also sick. She had a serious heart condition, which was giving her a great deal of trouble. Her condition had begun to worry Dave and he was now acting in a supervisory role to her in spite of his own serious heart condition. In about the third year of their marriage, Sue passed away.

Now, in his late eighties, David was also beginning to show signs of weariness. The stroke had left his right side weakened so that he dragged his left foot when he walked. My hunch is that his first wife's illness and subsequent death, and the stress that grew out of his recent series of life changes, weighed heavily upon him. In 1996, with his death, I lost a great friend.

Postscript: In the mid 1990's, I was busy helping to prepare both of my daughters for their weddings. Kimberly was engaged to Master Sergeant Aubrey C. Myers, U.S. Air Force, stationed in Alaska. There wedding was scheduled for June 10, 1995. Leslie was engaged to Daniel Morgan Ramsey of Dover, Delaware. Their wedding was scheduled for September 23, 1995.

Leslie and Danny's wedding was held at Leslie's church, St. Paul United Methodist Church, Trenton, New Jersey. An open invitation was extended to all members of St. Paul to attend the wedding. However, at the reception, only those church members who were close friends of the family were invited. Dr. David Fluck was among these friends. His escort was his twenty-three year old granddaughter. At the reception, she made a request to speak to me in private when it was convenient. When I granted her request, she asked me one question: "Miss Elsie, why didn't you marry Pop Pop? I was so hoping you would!" I was both warmed by her words, and saddened that David and I hadn't worked things out many years earlier, before his stroke took place.

Influential People: Mentors and Role Models

My Grandmother – Allie Richardson

As a youngster, I learned how to converse quite effectively with my grandparents. When I was very small (between five and seven years old), there were times when my grandmother and I would walk in the woods among trees and talk. I asked many questions about odd stones that I found on the ground; about flowers and plants I had picked and given to my grandmother to hold; and about the streaks of sunlight that pushed their way through the trees on their journey to the earth. My grandmother listened and responded appropriately. These private sessions in the woods gave my young mind and imagination opportunity to grow and expand. Those woods, and my curious spirit, will always be connected.

My Pop-Pop – Emzy Richardson

My Pop-pop cuddled and babied me. I was a little girl – a small girl at that, because I weighed only five pounds at birth – therefore, my grandfather was very protective of me since birth. I was also the first grandchild and my grandfather wanted to keep me always. I responded to this love by sitting on his lap and carrying on a constant conversation with him as often as I could. When I was old enough, I read portions of the newspaper to him also. He became quite ill when I was eight years old, and passed away when I was ten. His death had a serious emotional effect upon me, and has affected me for many years. I felt his love; the love of a senior parent.

Mrs. Rochelle Vinson

When I was six years old, I left the Wilson's Mills Elementary School for Colored Children and was transferred to the Short Journey Elementary School for Colored Children on Highway 210. I was in second grade. For the next six years, I spent every school day with Mrs. Rochelle Vinson and her daughter, Ione. Mrs. Rochelle, Miss Ione's stepmother, also played the role of mother to me. Wherever Miss Rochelle went, I went and where she slept, I slept. I even spent a summer's vacation at Sedalia Institute, Oxford, North Carolina with Mrs. Rochelle. I was referred to as Mrs. Vinson's "little girl," a title I carried even into adulthood. Being in the company of teachers and educators every school day for six years had a positive effect upon my life. I wanted to become a teacher.

My Mother, Ruth L. McIntosh

My mother was a woman with focus, goals, ambition, determination and heart. She was not afraid to tackle a problem and conquer it, despite whatever the odds were against her. Single-handedly, she raised three daughters and set them on positive courses that took them into productive professions. My mother demonstrated her love and respect for humankind by working continuously, despite her illness, to take care of her parents, her sister Nellie, and her own children. She was deeply religious and supportive of her church (Bethel AME on 135th Street in New York City) and she demonstrated her belief in her fellow man. She also served on the usher board and the choir at Bethel. My work ethic is similar: I was an educator for 49 years, and now I serve my fellow man in a variety of services as a volunteer.

The Barrys

Following my second year at Kittrell, I went home to New York. My plans for the next couple of years were already well established. I still owed Kittrell College a great deal of money for the two years I had attended college.

Finding a suitable job that would enable me to pay to Kittrell a given amount of money each month, secondly, to provide financial support to my mother each week; thirdly, to meet my own personal needs, would not be an easy task. I spent several weeks looking for a job, but was not successful in finding one that would pay enough money to meet my debt, and ongoing needs. Even though I had no special skills, I was bright and intelligent enough to successfully handle governmental jobs such as filing and office clerking. Doors were closed to me, I feel because of my race, and I was unable to find such work. So I settled for a sleep-in job at a Jewish home in Kew Gardens, New York.

The young family I worked for was the Barrys – Paul, Amy, and their two-year old daughter, Judy. Paul was a successful businessman who was part of a firm in downtown Manhattan. Amy was a stay-at-home wife and mother.

I was only nineteen years old when I went to live with the Barrys as their sleep-in maid. Paul Barry's connection to Hollywood brought many celebrities to the home. I saw them and assisted Amy in preparing for their arrival when necessary. But my principal job was caring for Judy, their two-year old daughter. I recall one very important Hollywood celebrity who visited their home. It was Lenny Heyton, who was a white Jewish producer and the first husband of Lena Horne. Lenny had come to urge Paul to come to Hollywood to become a full-fledged movie star. Paul had already done bit parts in the movie industry and was urged by certain friends of his to enter the movie business on a full-time basis. But it appeared that Paul's feet were firmly planted in New York.

Amy, who was only ten years my senior, was my friend as well as my boss. So Amy and I often talked about many things. Therefore, I was particularly well informed about some aspects of the family. Over sixty years have now passed, and Amy and I still keep in touch with each other. She now lives in Boca Raton, Florida.

Living in a Jewish household immersed me in Jewish culture and cuisine. I still enjoy the Jewish foods to which I was introduced while working for the Barrys: babka, blintzes, Jewish pot roast, and specially prepared fish. I also became familiar with colorful Yiddish terms like, mensch, mishigas, oy, ganott and yenta.

A sleep-in job meant that the maid's work was never ended. The maid was available and was called on at any time to do any job. I did not cook, but did everything else. My major job was taking care of Judy. Every Thursday and every other Sunday, I went home to Manhattan and stayed with my mother and two sisters.

I kept focused on my ultimate goal, which was to complete my college education, so I regarded this sleep-in job as a means to an end. My immediate responsibility was to pay my education bill at Kittrell, apply for admission to another college, and to save some money in preparation for my new college home.

I remained out of college and worked for one full school year, 1942-1943, plus over summer.

Mildred and Joseph Bedford

Mildred and Joe Bedford were just the family couple I needed at that particular period of my life. My mother had met them when she visited Delaware State College (now Delaware State University) during Parent Day, when I was a student there. I lived in their home when I was hired as the Social Studies teacher at Booker T. Washington Junior High School. They were also teachers, and Joe was the principal of a school in Harrington, Delaware. Both were true friends, but they were also my social counselors, my protectors, my advisors, my encouragers, and my parents. I respected them, listened to their advice and obeyed them. I learned these values at home and they were reinforced in the Bedford home.

Mrs. Genevieve Wisner

Mrs. Genevieve Wisner adopted me as her surrogate daughter during my senior year at college. She was a professor in the Music Department and the Director of the Choir at Delaware State College. She and her four sons had moved east from their home in Denver, Colorado to settle in Wilmington, Delaware. She had no daughters of her own, so my presence gave her the experience of having a daughter. Mrs. Wisner was quite civic minded and held membership in several organizations that promoted the well-being of people, especially the African-American population. One of these organizations was the National Organization of Negro Women, founded by Dr. Mary McCleod Bethune. She attended the conference in Washington, DC and took me with her.

She encouraged me to develop my singing ability and made me the principal soloist in the college choir. I also held membership in several civic organizations, and become a community activist. I expanded my singing ability, and was offered a voice fellowship to the Westminster Choir College in Princeton, New Jersey. I became a concert artist, a soloist, and also spent six summers with the Columbia University Teachers College Summer Chorus.

Mrs. Beatrice Henry

Mrs. Henry was a very sophisticated lady and was married to one of the three black dentists in Dover, Delaware, a small town of approximately 30,000 people. She was also a professor in the Music Department at Delaware State College and was the church organist at Whatcoat Methodist Episcopal Church in Dover. The Henrys had no children, so I became one of the young adults in the town that Mrs. Henry spent quality time with. I soon became the major church soloist. I spent many hours with Mrs. Henry learning new music and taking voice lessons. Mrs. Henry and I kept in touch with each other for many years after I left Dover, Delaware. When Mrs. Henry passed away in the mid-1980's, I attended the services at Delaware State College. I continued her love of music and became church soloist at my church, St. Paul United Methodist Church, Trenton, New Jersey.

Mrs. Bernice Munce

Occasionally, during a period of "quiet time," Mrs. Munce would say to me, "You are like the daughter I never had." Naturally, I was delighted, for I regarded Mrs. Munce as the smartest person I had ever met. Mrs. Munce was a person with power and influence. Beginning as a Social Studies teacher at Junior No. 5, she rose to be Superintendent of the Trenton School System. She also used her influence to upgrade and promote capable African-American educators where possible. I was in the right place at the right time. I was a single parent with two young children and a new resident of the City of Trenton. Mrs. Munce was impressed by the very positive reputation I had developed as a classroom teacher at Junior No. 5, so she set up opportunities for me to advance within the system. I did advance and made substantial progress in education.

Mrs. Lottie Dinkins

When I was invited to be the keynote speaker at the public meeting in New York City of the National Association of Registered Nurses of the United States and Africa at Hotel Roosevelt in 1980, Mrs. Munce suggested that I contact Mrs. Lottie Dinkins (mother of the young man who became Mayor David Dinkins) and ask her to help me write the address. I did and we became very close friends. Mrs. Dinkins also suggested that she would like to be my mentor, which pleased me very much.

Between 900-1,000 people attended the public meeting in Manhattan, New York, including the Mayor and other public and state officials. The Governor was invited to attend but sent a representative instead. I received a standing ovation from the audience; the speech was a huge success.

Under the guidance of Mrs. Munce, and supported by Mrs. Dinkins, my popularity grew educationally and even socially. I was a very protective mother and made sure that my children were always properly supported and lived in the best environment. Because of my very busy schedule, I declined attendance and participation in many of the social events to which I was invited. This also included my beloved Alpha Kappa Alpha Sorority.

Miss Ione Vinson

From age six, I traveled to school each day with Miss Ione Vinson and her mother, Mrs. Rochelle Vinson, but the tight relationship developed after Miss Ione retired from teaching. Following my job teaching summer school at Trenton State College (The College of New Jersey) in early August, my daughters and I went to Wilson's Mills to spend time with family members – Bro Purl and "Cuz" Ione – before our school opened in September. After the death of Bro Purl (Richardson) and the destruction of the Richardson home, I continued to go south and spend a few weeks each summer with Miss Ione. "Cuz" Ione, who never married and had no children, looked forward to our summer visits. It was like a mother/daughter relationship, and it lasted for years. Ione was a very intelligent woman. She earned a master's degree in elementary education from Teachers College, Columbia University, and taught school for forty-seven years. It was Ione who encouraged me to write my first book, *Smalltown Strutters.*

As Ione advanced in age, and her health began to fail, she turned all her personal business over to me and trusted me to take care of her. I did and made sure that Ione had the best attention that could be provided. Ione was satisfied. Eventually, she passed away at age 93.

Amy and Joseph Evans

Amy graduated from Delaware State one year ahead of me. We were friends at college and our friendship continued. After graduation, we both took teaching jobs in Delaware. Amy got married after a few years to Joe Evans, who worked at the shipyard in Philadelphia. She soon resigned from her teaching position in Delaware and joined her husband in Philadelphia. She returned to school at Temple University in Philadelphia and completed her master's program in social work. Amy then became a social worker for the City of Philadelphia.

Camden, New Jersey is right across the Delaware River from Philadelphia. During the years when I was having marital problems, I lived in Camden, just a few miles from Amy and Joe and their two sons. Amy and Joe were very sympathetic and became very supportive of me and the children.

During the time of my marital problems, Douglas, a motorman with New York City Transit Authority, was spending most of his time in New York. The children, Leslie (3), and Kimberly (an infant) and I, stayed at our home in Camden. Amy and Joe were available whenever we needed them and tremendously helpful. As Kimberly's godparents, they played a major role in her life. My friendship with this couple grew in the years to follow. To me, they felt like blood relatives. Amy passed away in 1993, and Joe in the year 2000.

Dr. D'Arce`

Dr. D'Arce` was my French teacher in Kittrell. Though of African-American or Mulatto descent, he was a real Frenchman, born and educated in France. When I met him, he was of advanced age, a grandfatherly type that immediately drew me to him. We became very close friends. In fact, at 18, I was truly like his granddaughter.

His academic influence upon me was also profound. I became almost French! When I left Kittrell after two years of study, I was able to carry on a complete conversation in French, and was able to read it as well.

Dr. D'Arce` encouraged and promoted this proficiency among his students, and I was among his brightest. After graduating from Delaware State and getting a job teaching social studies at Booker T. Washington Junior High School in Dover, Delaware, I saw Dr. D'Arce` again. He had retired from Kittrell. At this particular time, he was sent to Dover, Delaware as a member of the AME Conference Delegation. I did not know he was in the delegation, and was overjoyed and surprised when I located him. We spent as much time together as we could before he left. Dr. D'Arce` was accompanied by his granddaughter, who explained that they would be returning home to France in the near future. They did, but Dr. D'Arce` and I continued to keep in contact with each other. Before his death a few years later, he sent me a full-length photo of himself.

Bro Purl and Bro David: My Uncles

These two men were my mother's brothers. Each served as a disciplinarian to me in my formative and early teen years. However, each had a different understanding of its meaning and also how it should be administered. Regardless of how it was administered, each man had a positive, lasting effect upon my life. They helped direct my life along those pathways that led to constructive results.

Reverend Purl was a practicing AME minister. He saw his role as safe-guarding and protecting his mother, after the death of his father. He was the oldest child and it became a potential responsibility. The grandchildren (my sisters and I), saw him as a father figure and respected him as such. He lived right next door and was in and out of grandmom's home daily.

David, the younger uncle, was fun loving, carefree and jovial. He was quiet and never involved in an argumentative type conversation, but was usually involved in reading the newspaper or other academic materials of interest. He was also an alcoholic who spent every weekend under the influence of alcohol and in need of help and supervision from his nieces, especially me.

From these two uncles, I learned to respect authority and to obey the command. I also learned what patience meant, and how to apply it. I saw love and practiced it. I saw appreciation and practiced it. I learned that love is the true ingredient that holds our values together and that it can be covert and unspoken.

Dr. Ercell Watson

Dr. Ercell Watson and his family moved into Trenton a few years after I did when he was appointed Superintendent of the Trenton Public School System. He was the first African-American to serve in this capacity in the history of the school system. I was delighted to be among the many teachers who marched with placards in front of the Board of Education building in support of hiring Dr. Watson to fill this position. He proved to be an excellent administrator and developed programs necessary in education for the Trenton Public Schools. During his tenure of service I was invited to take a position at Trenton State College in the Department of Education Field Experience by Dr. Bernard Schwartz. Because I was doing so well in curriculum and teacher training in Trenton's public school system, I was not particularly interested in going to the college to teach. So when I received the invitation letter from Dr. Schwartz, I showed it to Mrs. Munce, but also told her that I was not interested in teaching at the college level.

Mrs. Munce advised me to speak with Dr. Watson, School Superintendent, before rejecting the invitation. So I did. Dr. Watson informed me that it was one of the highest honors that could be offered and I should be proud. He encouraged me to take the position. He would give me a three-year professional leave of absence from the system, and would hold my job open. However, at the beginning of the fourth year, the job would be offered to someone else. But that three-year time span could be my opportunity to see whether or not I enjoyed being a college professor.

I took Dr. Watson's advice, accepted the invitation to teach at the college. I left the Trenton Public Schools the fall of 1971, stayed 21 years at Trenton State College and rose to the rank of an Associate Professor before my retirement in 1990. I never regretted the move. In all, I was in the business of education for thirty-four years in the State of New Jersey and New York, and had spent an additional fifteen years in the State of Delaware.

Walter Grandy/Road Not Taken #1

In the mid 1980's, the public school system of the City of Durham, North Carolina was having its share of problems. These problems were apparent, especially to Walter Grandy. A high school teacher, Grandy was one of the members of the more influential African-American families in Durham and someone who, along with many others, wanted to see school problems remedied. He was born in Durham and followed in the footsteps of his community-activist parents. His brother, Dr. Clem Grandy and his two sisters, Mable and Mamie, teachers, all were movers and shakers.

Walter, who knew me through Cousin Ione Vinson of Wilson's Mills, called me in Trenton, early in the school year, about mid-September. Immediately following the usual greetings, he sprang the request. "We want you to run for Superintendent of Schools for the Durham Public School System. School board elections are next spring, in April, and we want your name on the ballot." I was stunned and delighted to have been asked. "Suppose I lose?" I remember saying. "You will not lose, we guarantee you will win that election."

A million questions raced through my mind. Was I ready to move to a new city? Did I want to leave college work? How would I manage Leslie and Kimberly who were now in their early teens? Suppose I did not turn out to be an effective administrator and lost the job? Suppose the college would not release me and would fire me if I left?

I told my department chair and the Dean of the School of Education, Dr. Ollio, about the offer. Both were quite excited about it. They both explained how my taking this post would have a positive effect on the School of Education, as well as the College. They both urged me to take advantage of the opportunity.

Dean Ollio explained that the college would give me a three-year leave of absence as a Participating Professor in Education Administration. However, I realized that a period of three years would not be long enough for me to make an effective difference in the educational system of this city. So I met with the Dean in a follow-up meeting and gave him a skeleton outline I would follow to correct the problem the city was experiencing. I felt that I would need five years to do the job well; the first year to study the system and become acquainted with the personnel, the system problems, the source and/or causes of the problems and begin to discuss the same with connections. The second year I would begin to replace/remove problems through observations and suggestions and meetings with appropriate personnel. The third year: have new programs, policies, personnel in place. The fourth year: observe progress, refine, adjust, and eliminate where needed. And the fifth year, evaluation completed, measurements done, the system should be working well. The Board of Education would make a decision, based on recommendations and observations, whether or not to approve or adopt my program.

Ultimately, with some regret, I did not accept the offer to run for Superintendent of Schools in Durham. I concluded that three years simply would not give me enough time to design, implement and evaluate my program for the school system.

Mrs. Elizabeth Gordon/Road Not Taken #2

A few years later, I also received an invitation to serve my country at the national level.

The National Teacher Corps was in need of a competent administrator to run its program in the Virgin Islands. The Washington, D.C. headquarters advertised through a search committee for such a person. My name was submitted by Mrs. Elizabeth Gordon Director of Teacher Corps, Northeast Region.

Elizabeth became acquainted with me from a previous engagement. When the Teachers Corps Program was brought to Trenton, I was selected as one of the five master teachers/team leaders to work directly with them. Thirty-five young, prospective teachers were in the program to be divided among the team leaders. Team leaders were given seven or eight students to lead. I was given eight. I was told that I did commendable work in the program. This involvement opened doors for me, and my name was pushed up to the national level.

I received a phone call from Mrs. Gordon informing me that my name was now in the pool of applicants for the Virgin Islands post and that I had the best chance of winning. She wanted to know whether or not I would accept. Again, I had to examine, weigh and balance all circumstances pertaining to this position in the Virgin Islands.

My children were still young and I was still a single parent. Leslie was fifteen now, and Kimberly was twelve. I was having no serious problems with my daughters and believed that it was because I was able to manage closely their academic and social life. I wondered: Could this degree of management continue in a different location?

After several conferences via phone with Elizabeth, I learned what the job in the Virgin Islands would involve. The program would be based at the three largest islands – St. Croix, St. Thomas, and St. Maarten. On each island, students would be placed under the direct supervision of master teachers. My responsibility would be to promote the program, supervise master teachers, coordinate content and activities, and evaluate work being done on each island. In order to efficiently carry out my responsibilities, I would be island hopping daily.

Under these circumstances, the girls would be left alone a good deal of time, unsupervised. Also, much of the time they would be on their own to find answers to questions, places to go, things to do, and people to lead them. I was unwilling to leave my children unsupervised with so many unknowns, which may or may not have had negative effects upon their lives. So I declined the invitation. The decision I had to make was in the best interests of my children and their protection, so there were few enduring regrets.

Dr. Luna I. Mishoe

When I was eighteen years old, I went to Kittrell College, Kittrell, North Carolina, as a freshman. I was opening the door to new and interesting eras of my young life. One of them was the opportunity to meet new and interesting personalities who would make an impact. Dr. Luna I. Mishoe was one of these personalities. Neither of us was aware of the interlocking of our lives to come.

Dr. Mishoe was chairperson of the Department of math at Kittrell. He was a graduate of Morehouse College, and had completed his master's program in physics at Howard University. Now in his late twenties, he was heading up the Math Department at Kittrell.

It was Dr. Mishoe who got me interested in math. He recognized my potential in this area, and encouraged me to select math as my major. I had listened and followed his guidance. I took several courses in math, advanced math, and also physics. This strong freshman and sophomore foundation in math enabled me to secure a minor in math at graduation from Delaware State.

After my sophomore year, I left Kittrell and continued my education at Delaware State College in 1943-44 and 1944-45. I graduated with a double major and a double minor. They were the teaching of social studies and the teaching of English, and the teaching of French and the teaching of math.

I was employed as a social studies teacher at Booker T. Washington Jr. High School, Dover, Delaware upon graduation.

Several years later, in the mid-1950's, I learned that a new professor by the name of Dr. Luna I. Mishoe, was coming to Delaware State College to work in the area of administration. My interest grew as I wondered whether or not this was my math professor from Kittrell. I had to find out. I called the administration office at the college for information and learned that this current Dr. Mishoe was indeed my former math teacher. After getting his office phone number, I called him and introduced myself. His surprise and joy in meeting an old friend mirrored my feelings.

Mr. Mishoe was now Dr. Mishoe. He had received a prestigious fellowship to complete his doctoral work at Oxford University in England. Meanwhile, he had received several awards and citations for his work in physics and community services. He had also gotten married and was the father of four children – two sons and two daughters.

I had also continued my education. Following graduation, I enrolled at Teachers College, Columbia University to pursue a master's program in 1948. I completed the program in 1951.

As the opportunities arose, I gladly introduced Dr. Mishoe to my friends, as my former professor. They considered it "so cool."

Dr. Mishoe's upward climb in the world of academia continued. The college was about to begin its search for a new president, since the current one was about to retire. Dr. Mishoe seized the opportunity to advance his academic career by becoming a candidate for this position. In the late 1960's, the Board of Trustees of Higher Education, State of

Delaware, appointed Dr. Mishoe President of Delaware State College. Dr. Luna I. Mishoe became the president of the college and remained in this position for the next twenty-two years.

When Dr. Mishoe became president of Delaware State, many changes had occurred in my life also. I had gotten married, left the State of Delaware, became a mother, got a divorce, earned a Ph.D., and became a college professor.

I was also a very active alumnus of Delaware State College. I made annual monetary contributions to the college and attended certain college-wide activities when my schedule allowed. The presence also enabled President Mishoe to keep in contact with me.

I received a personal letter from Dr. Mishoe in Spring of 1983 requesting me to be the keynote speaker for Parent Day Program at the college. Of course, I answered in the affirmative and was the speaker at the college on May 23, 1983.

Dr. Mishoe was a dedicated supporter of the National Association for Equal Education Opportunities (NAFEO), whose membership was composed of the historically black colleges and universities of the United States, as well as all other black colleges and universities. Many community colleges are also members. Every four years, the presidents, chancellors, or provosts selected a chair of the organization from among their ranks. Dr. Mishoe was chosen chair person of this prestigious, powerful organization in 1985.

I was now Associate Professor of Education at Trenton State College and had joined the college in 1971. Every year, Dr. Ollio, Dean of the School of Education, made funds available for me to attend the NAFEO Conference in Washington, D.C. to represent Trenton State College and the School of Education. Even though I associated and interacted with delegates representing the many colleges and universities throughout the United States, my main family of associates was the delegation from Delaware State University. Dr. Mishoe always headed that delegation.

The four-day NAFEO Conference, which began on Thursday and ran through Sunday afternoon, at the Hilton Hotel, Washington, D.C., was filled with action. There were continuous workshops of variation, mini-conferences, exhibits, presentations, keynotes, dramas, etc. However, one of the highlights of the conference is the citations/awards banquet held on Saturday afternoon-evening. Individuals who have met the criteria/definition of service to humankind in its varied forms and levels are honored. The individuals are chosen from every walk of life and do not necessarily have to be associated with historically black colleges. The Delaware State University selected five individuals to be so honored. I was one of those five individuals in 1987.

In a private conversation with me, Dr. Mishoe commended me on my achievements, my contributions to education, my humanitarian involvement, and told me that he was very proud of me. I was elated.

Dr. Mishoe's insistence that I, as a young college student, could do advanced math and physics helped train my mind and encouraged me to continue to reach my highest potential.

The Parkers – William & Robert

I met Dr. William (Bill) Parker following one of his presentations at Trenton Central High School in Trenton. Dr. Parker was well known for his presentations. They were humorous, yet filled with pertinent information that applied to both black and white Americans. If Dr. Bill Parker was the speaker, people came from far and near to hear him. Listeners often became participants, as well, which elevated the meaning in the dialogue and provided both laughter and humor. On some special occasions, Bill's brother, Dr. Robert (Bob) Parker would join him in the presentation and the audience would then get a double dose of information and humor. The brothers were African-Americans.

Both of the Parker brothers were working at Educational Testing Service (ETS), Princeton, New Jersey when I met them. William was the Director of Information and Minority Affairs for Educational Testing Service (ETS). Robert was Director of Testing Security. His job was to defend and protect the validity of the tests through court appearances as well as special sessions or defense. In the implementation of their services, both brothers did a great deal of traveling. Both brothers were learned gentlemen with earned doctorates in education administration.

In my search for resource information and materials to use in my class of graduate students, I decided that the Parker brothers would be an excellent choice. In the master's program at Trenton State College, I taught the course entitled, "Curriculum Construction and Staff Development," required of all students seeking certification in education administration or management. This was an evening course, which met for two hours every Tuesday and Thursday evening. To augment and enrich the content of my class, I used resource materials where appropriate. I decided that the Parker brothers would be an excellent asset to my class. So they were invited to participate, and graciously accepted. Their participation became so well known that former students, as well as visitors, filled my class to hear them. Student participation, as well as questions from the audience were always a part of the two-hour sessions. One question from the students that should be mentioned here is as follows, "As I was taught that black people still carry much of their African heritage, is it true one of the things they do is pull off their clothes when they enter their home and remain naked until they leave home?" This ridiculous question brought on laughter and applause. However, when all was quiet, the Parker brothers provided a fitting answer. Their composure and thoughtful answer resulted in thunderous applause.

Although I made offers to pay the Parkers for their services, they never accepted payment. I made it clear, however, that I would be willing to help them whenever I could. My offer was accepted immediately. I soon realized that I was an on-going participant in the Parker team. Here is how it worked: I would get a call from one of the Parker brothers, usually Bill, telling me that they were invited to make a presentation at so and so school, at a particular time on a given date, with a particular theme. I was asked to handle the theme development part of the presentation. Since I was a single parent, my presentations were usually during the day when my children were at school. The other person who became a team member was Hugh Strayborn, Director of the Division of Guidance and Counseling, Trenton Public School System. This very influential team was quite active in central and northern New Jersey and also Bucks County in Pennsylvania. When Dr. Bill Parker accepted the position of Professor of Black History and Director of Department of Minority Affairs at the University of Kentucky, the Parker team became inactive.

My membership on this team forced me to get control of my emotions immediately. I learned to manage quite well the fear that always gripped me when I was called to perform. My self-confidence deepened and I knew that the team members were always there to fill in when and if needed. I was also very proud to be a member of such an outstanding and learned group. As I was the only female, the guys were just very protective.

The Hang-Out Gang

The "place to be" was the home of the McIntosh girls. It was a "right on" place with the kind of environment that put everybody at ease. Guys and gals would hang out, which meant to argue, to disagree, to agree, to discuss, to debate, and to evaluate topics of the day. Sometimes, the gang played cards, period.

The "hang out" participants were just ordinary people and yet, we were very special people; young people in pursuit of our dreams and goals, but who had also come together in this place at this time. These guys and girls who met were:

- Morris White – Manager, Mt. Morris Park Hospital, Doctoral candidate, New York University;
- Napoleon Pinckney – Second year medical student, New York Medical Center, Albany, New York;
- Mr. Claude Moore - Worker in services, City of New York;
- Granville Hay – City College Graduate, Management of Professional Offices (dentists);
- Elena Burstein, Ph.D. – Post Doctoral Studies, Behavioral Sciences, a European from Austria; Columbia University Student;
- Elsie Ellen McIntosh – Teachers College, Columbia University student in Masters' Program;
- James Marshburn – High School Graduate, World War II Veteran, full-time employee U.S. Post Office, my sister Allie's boyfriend and fiancé.
- Romeo Cherot – Rhodes Scholar, Reporter, Voice of America, Radio Free Europe.

What brought these minds of varying interests and pursuits together? What was the staying power that held them together for a time? How did such a young group benefit the participants? How did such a group get started?

The Hang-Out Gang just sort of materialized. It had no formal place or organizer. Some members of the gang were acquaintances, some were also friends already, like "Nap" and Morris. Others were interested in establishing a courtship or relationship with me like Grandville Hay and Romeo Cherot. Some, I was interested in, like Napoleon, but he was interested in Elena. Elena was also interested in Napoleon. Mr. Claude was happily married, and the oldest member, but enjoyed being in the gang of young people. James Marshburn was engaged to my sister Allie. He had moved into our home and they were planning their wedding.

Card playing was a minor activity of the gang, but enjoyable. Partners were chosen randomly. This meant whoever was available and desired to play became partners. Refreshments, such as food and alcohol were not prepared or served. If the gang so desired to have beer and some food refreshments during the course of the evening, the "guys" would collect funds from each other and someone would go out and purchase what was ordered.

This was not a drinking party, but a grouping of intellectuals who had information about, and many solutions to, the pressing and perplexing problems of the day.

The discussions were exhilarating, some times heated, always exciting. No one got angry and no one went away mad. But every one went away fulfilled. Hay's statement about the meetings of the Hang-Out Gang summarized everyone's feeling. "It's the place to be. I wouldn't miss these meetings for nothing in the world."

Dr. Bernard Schwartz

Dr. Bernard Schwartz was the kind of influential, powerful friend everybody needs, who is in the right place at the right time. Bernie, the name his friends gave him, was chair of the Department of Educational Field Experiences (later changed to the Department of Education Administration and Secondary Education) at Trenton State Teachers College. This Department established teaching content/subject matter and experiences for those juniors who were secondary majors and placed them in schools during both their junior and senior years. There, the students did their practice-teaching under the direct supervision of a cooperating teacher.

During these years, I was a young social studies teacher at Trenton Junior High No. 5. I had made a positive impression upon my students who made favorable statements to their parents about me. Mrs. Bernice Munce, Assistant Director of Curriculum and Staff Development, Trenton School System, was also quite impressed with my performance as a teacher. So she recommended me to Dr. Schwartz as a cooperating teacher.

I served as cooperating teacher for the college for several years. During this time I was called upon to demonstrate my teaching techniques and behaviors with my students one evening at Junior No. 5. Many parents, as well as college professors and students were in attendance.

When Dr. Schwartz and Mrs. Munce brought the Teacher Corp Program to the Trenton Public School System, five master teachers from the school system were needed to perform as team leaders to the thirty-two teacher interns in the program. I was one of these five master teachers selected for the program.

Dr. Schwartz and Mrs. Munce brought to the school system another Federal/State program that required the cooperation of both the college and the public school system for implementation and that was the Career Opportunities Program (COP). COP was a step-up program where students were aided by the public school system and the college to climb the education ladder and complete both their high school education and their college education as well. This enabled para-professionals to become professionals. I was appointed Assistant Director and Mrs. Daisy Morgan was appointed director of this program. The program lasted two years, but was an important starting point for the journey of many individuals on their way to becoming professionals.

Dr. Schwartz and I got to know each other quite well. I was a cooperating teacher in his department; a master teacher in the Teacher Corps; and helped to direct the COP program's teacher training component. My own growth and development in professional education and teacher training were accelerating, and my students and colleagues held me in high esteem.

Six of the nine New Jersey state colleges had gotten their start as teachers colleges, also called "normal schools" in their infancy. For a very long time, all graduates of the original six institutions were entering teaching. Until the late 1960's, those New Jersey students seeking a four-year public college or university education, but not planning careers in education, had few in-state alternatives; Rutgers University was one highly regarded option.

At that time, New Jersey experienced a huge exodus of students graduating high school in-state but bound for out-of-state colleges and universities. This is still the case today although the situation has improved somewhat. One of the most compelling concerns to be addressed in this context was the need to move from a single purpose (education) state college constellation to a set of multipurpose institutions. The multipurpose institutions would provide an array of academic programs to students who did not expect to become teachers. Additionally, it was understood that there was a need to provide students with challenging academic programs that would be respected and which would attract well-prepared students. A proposal to the state higher education authority, put forth by the college administration, that Trenton State College become a sort of "test site" for this transformation, was accepted.

In fulfillment of the college's new, overarching goals, existing programs at the college in teacher education were revitalized and expanded. The new Department of Educational Administration and Secondary Education oversaw the training of all secondary education majors in the liberal arts, theatre, the sciences, and all branches of math. Training began in the student's junior year at the college. For an entire semester, the student was involved in what was known as Junior Professional Experience (JPE). It was a comprehensive study of the dynamics of teaching. One of two days per week, the student participated in a two-hour seminar conducted by his/her education professor. Then three days were spent in the classroom of a participating school under the supervision of a cooperating teacher who allowed the student to apply the teaching technique taught by the college professor. The more assertive and cooperative the student was, the more responsibility the cooperating teacher gave him/her. Therefore, close to the end of the semester, the student was allowed to fully control one or two classes per week with the cooperating teacher supervising.

The college professor was required to meet several times per week with the cooperating teacher, as well as observe the college student perform in the classroom.

In the senior year of the student teaching, one half semester, or eight weeks, were spent in classroom performance. If at all possible, the senior returned to the same school and co-op teacher to complete senior student-teaching requirements.

The college supervising professor was expected to make at least six to eight full-day observational visits to the school per student per half-semester.

Dr. Schwartz wanted me to join his staff and become a professor in the Department of Secondary Education. He discussed the matter with me and extended the invitation. I was hesitant. As a single parent, I was already secure in my position with the Trenton Public School System and did not wish to take chances on jobs that might create insecurity. But, I was encouraged by Mrs. Bernice Munce and Dr. Ercell Watson, School Superintendent to go to the college and become a professor. And so I did in 1971, and stayed there twenty-one years.

Dr. Bernard Schwartz was that mentor that moved me from public education into higher education. He gave me the opportunity to become a college professor, which demanded a doctorate. He assured me that I could do doctoral work. He became a member of the doctoral committee and he worked closely with me throughout the entire grueling experience. I am forever grateful to him.

Paul Shelly – My Caucasian Godson

When Paul came to St. Paul United Methodist Church in the late 1970's, he was a young man just a handful of years out of graduate school. After a few conversations with him, I detected an openness of mind and refreshing aspects of his personality that I admired. We soon developed a mother/son relationship that has continued to grow and mellow over the years.

When I learned that Paul was visiting several churches in the area in search of a church home, I, along with other church members, encouraged Paul to remain at St. Paul for a few years to find out whether or not he would wish to join. He did so; and later joined St. Paul.

Immediately, he became very active by joining several committees. Some of the committees and groups that Paul joined were those in which I was already active. They included the committees on Missions and Outreach, a community organization getting started in Trenton's West Ward, and Trenton Ecumenical Area Ministry (TEAM).

Paul's intellect, abundance of information, dry wit, and humility fascinated me. I soon discovered that his range of intellect was quite broad and I could easily discuss with him a variety of topics. Therefore, I sought his advice on several important issues, both personal and educational.

Over the several years of our friendship, Paul has played an active role in many of my affairs. He was the photographer at the wedding of my daughter, Leslie Jean. When I was honored by the Community Educational Advisory Council (CEAC), with a banquet, Paul was one of the major speakers. And it was Paul who wrote a "protest letter" for publication in support of me during a particularly difficult matter involving racism.

I was absolutely delighted when, in the Spring of 1997, Paul nominated me for a brand new award offered by Ramapo College of New Jersey, honoring the State of New Jersey's unsung heroes. Although I did not receive the top award, as a runner-up, Paul and I received a special invitation to the college. We had a smashing evening which included an opportunity to meet the college president as well as Russ and Angelica Berrie, the celebrated sponsors of the Russ Berrie Award for Making a Difference.

During my retirement years, I decided to develop my writing talent by publishing a book about the small town in North Carolina where I lived when I was a small child. I needed Paul's advice, and talked the matter over with him. Paul encouraged me to go ahead with the project and volunteered to serve as my editor. Under Paul's editorial guidance and generous supervision, I am completing my third book. Paul's right hand was always there to make sure that all aspects of the books were done right, and his long-time influence is still a guiding force in my life.

Paul has a lovely wife whose name is Susan, and I am the "godmother" to this lovely couple.

The Capones

Early in the 1980's, I was introduced to Ana, a friend of my sister Allie, her husband and their two children.

My sister Allie and Ana became close over a period of several years. They had worked together as nurses in the same hospital. Ana was born in Puerto Rico, of African-Hispanic descent. She was a nursing supervisor in the New York City medical system. Al was Italian, born in Brooklyn, New York of the Capone Family.

Their two children were photogenic; both had appeared in group movie scenes in New York. However, the parents were very protective of their children.

Ana had an old-fashioned sewing machine that she had inherited from her grandmother in Puerto Rico. The machine had been shipped to her home in Brooklyn, New York. When she learned that she was terminally ill, she wanted to give the machine to someone who would keep it. Allie told Ana about me, my teenage girls, and discussed the possibility of having the machine presented to my family. So Ana and her family came to Trenton, gave me the Singer sewing machine, and spent the day. We remained acquainted, however, Ana passed away a few years later.

After Anna passed away, Al kept in contact with Allie and her husband Jimmy, and me.

I never will forget a special evening spent with Al years later. My daughters, Leslie and Kimberly, and I visited Allie and Jimmy in Teaneck, New Jersey over the weekend. Al knew that we would be there and he insisted upon taking me out to dinner and entertainment during my stay. We went to Manhattan to an area known as "Little Italy." This was a very private club, filled with people speaking Italian and some English. Al was greeted with great respect. We were seated in a private area with a special waiter to serve us. I may have been the only African-American there, and truly enjoyed the attention given to Al and me.

Al and I are still friends and call each other occasionally.

Interesting Experiences and People in the State of New Jersey

Community Educational Advisory Council (CEAC)

CEAC (Community Educational Advisory Council) was a community-based organization whose objective was to enable parents to work/deal more effectively with the school system on behalf of their children. Many African American parents in this tight-knit neighborhood in the town of Hamilton, New Jersey were dissatisfied with the way their children were treated at school. They had complained continuously to the teachers, to the school principals, and even to the Board of Education without discernable results. African American children were harassed at school and after school. But they were especially harassed; it was felt, by those teachers who consistently sent them home from school daily for arriving at school late only one or two minutes. These school suspensions lasted from one to nine days, and, only too often, it was the same child or set of children.

Poppy Wilson, Executive Director of Hamilton Neighborhood Service Center, told me about this problem. He explained in detail just how upset the parents were about it. He wanted to know whether or not I, as an educator and member of the Center's board, had some ideas that might be helpful to the parents. I said I thought so. Of course, I had had my own run-ins with teachers and administrators in Hamilton when my children were attending school there.

Following further conversation with Poppy and others at the Hamilton Neighborhood Service Center, a meeting was called. I was present and concerned parents of the neighborhood were in attendance. Following a robust discussion, Poppy scheduled another community meeting at the Center and stated that Dr. Collins would form an organization of concerned parents.

Many parents and interested community persons showed up for this next gathering. Poppy opened the meeting and then turned to me to preside over it.

After some discussion, a focus on our direction and goals began to emerge. Under my direction and suggestions, an organization was formed and the group unanimously accepted the name "Community Education Advisory Council". The organization became known as CEAC, and I was regarded as its founder and elected as its first president.

The following mission statement became CEAC's guiding force:

> The Community Educational Advisory Council shall be a community-based organization whose membership shall consist of Hamilton Township citizens. The organization originated out of express concern of parents who felt limited in their abilities to assist their youngsters in meeting certain personal and academic problems which seem to be inhibitive to proper educational growth and development. These concerns include such broad areas as the following: proper study habits, career choices, academic programs, discipline, testing and student placement, absenteeism, suspension and expulsion, going to college, etc. The parents needed workable and satisfactory ways of helping their children and enabling them to be successful individuals.

Long-range goals, which would give strength and direction to the organization, were established by the group. These goals included:

1. To broaden and sharpen community awareness of the educational process in the Hamilton Township school system;

2. To increase community involvement in the local activities that determine educational policies and procedures;
3. To motivate the community and assist it in taking advantage of the educational networking system available to the citizens and families of Hamilton Township.

Another unwritten law, but major, objective of the organization was to increase the membership. To be an effective organization, and reach as many homes as possible, joining the organization had to be easy and simple. To that end, it was agreed that any citizen of the township who was at least sixteen years of age and wished to make a positive contributions to the betterment of the educational system in Hamilton Township, may join the organization. A monetary contribution of one dollar per year is expected.

Membership in the organization grew steadily and leveled off at about twenty dedicated steadfast members. The following is a list of those steadfast working individuals:

1. Arthur Williamson
2. Sydney Andrews
3. Robert Batts
4. Gary Gray
5. John Harris
6. John Golden
7. Robert "Poppy" Wilson
8. Kenneth Jackson
9. B.J. Nelson
10. Mr. McKinsey, Guidance Counselor at Grice School in Hamilton, NJ.
11. Brenda Cusack
12. Barbara Ollarvia
13. Elsie M. Collins
14. Irene Paramoure
15. Patricia Vincent
16. Delores Nelson
17. Barbara Carthan
18. Grace Hodges
19. Carolyn Johnson

The young organization, now widely known as CEAC, decided to take some bold positive steps in the community to motivate the citizens and to show that CEAC really meant business. At least once a month, co-sponsored by Poppy and Kenny, we held a young people's dance/social time at the Center. There was no monetary charge, but all children had to be accompanied by one or more parent or parental representative. Many parents were in attendance, and naturally, there were many young people.

These social hours reintroduced parents to each other, as well as to the many neighborhood children.

In addition to the social hours, CEAC sponsored a number of workshops at the center. Parents and students participated and the meetings grew in attendance and substance. The following are some of the programs of special interest to parents:

1. Guidance Programs in the Hamilton Township School System;
2. Strengthening Communication Skills Between Parents and Teachers;
3. Criteria for Classification of Schools by the State of New Jersey;
4. Preparing for the Required Testing Programs;
5. The Year of the Child as Proclaimed by the United Nations; and
6. Preparing to Enter College.

When parents called for help from CEAC, because a child was in trouble, how should CEAC respond? A formula was developed by CEAC, which made it easy for both parents and the school to work through the problem and solve it. Here is how it worked:

1. I was the major contact person, and was the first person to be called;
2. Knowing which CEAC member was available to assist and investigate the situation; I called those members and explained the situation to them. Not less than four CEAC members were required for involvement. Up to ten members have been necessary for clearance and understanding by all parties affected, namely, the school system and the parents.

I was always in attendance at these meetings. CEAC discovered a situation where one student had been suspended from school 175 days over a period of four years.
These lost days were equivalent to the loss of one year of school. This evidence was damaging to a school system that has been assigned the responsibility by the state to protect and educate all of its children.

3. This committee of four/five individuals met with the parents and the student at their home, as soon as possible.
4. The student explained the problem – the entire problem, in detail, as well as the steps the school had taken to solve or punish the student for this problem. The student was also required to explain similar problems and his previous problems at the school, or with other teachers. Parents were also encouraged to participate in the discussion so that all information regarding this problem was absolutely clear to the entire committee.
5. I then contacted the school principal, explained CEAC's involvement, and asked for an opportunity to meet with the principal, the discipline officer, and the teacher involved. The principal set a date and informed the affected school personnel.
6. I called an emergency CEAC meeting. I updated the members of CEAC of the problem, the meeting with the student and parents, and the upcoming meeting at the school with administrative personnel and the teacher. CEAC members discussed the concerns and problems, and offered suggestions. Sometimes one or two additional parents would volunteer to attend the meeting at the school.
7. CEAC members met at the school with the personnel involved: namely, the principal, the school disciplinarian, the teacher, sometimes other teachers with a gripe, and the guidance counselor. Also in attendance, was the student with one or both parents.
8. The conference lasted one or two class periods. The principal, usually in his/her office or a neutral area, conducted the meeting.

The teachers explained the school requirements and expectations. Then pointed out how or where the student had not met school requirements, had broken discipline codes or laws, and had not lived up to school expectations. Given the facts they would state the type of punishment warranted.

The student explained his version of the total situation, his understanding of the discipline code and his ability and/or inability to adhere to it. Parents explained their understanding of the code and its application, whether just or unjust. CEAC members asked many, many questions that encouraged the administration to look at the daily application of the discipline codes/laws, and the specific ongoing daily, personal needs of the students, and teachers' attitudes, as well.

9. Following this meeting, the CEAC organization waited to hear from the principal of the school. I was always the contact person. Responses from the principal were usually prompt since the problem usually involved students having been suspended from school. Whatever the results were, I immediately called together the CEAC members who had met with the school personnel, and discussed the issue, before contacting parents of the students.
10. The CEAC committee met with the parents and the student and discussed, at length, the results. Strict discipline guidelines to govern the student's conduct and cooperation with the school system were established. It was strongly suggested that the practice of open-mindedness, fair play, tolerance and understanding become a requirement for school staff in treatment of students. CEAC also strongly requested multi-cultural materials be included in the school curriculum. A volunteer committee of parents, teachers and students often visited the schools to serve as a check-up system.

Soon, the positive effects of the CEAC organization began to spread throughout the community of African American citizens. The community was quite pleased. At the same time, an unfavorable attitude was exhibited by the central administration of the school system. These top administrators were the Superintendent of Schools, the Assistant Superintendent in Charge of Business and Finance, and the Assistant Superintendent in Charge of Curricular Revision and Staff Development. They labeled the organization, and especially me, as troublemakers who were interfering with the orderly process of school business.

However, they took no steps to stop me or to dismantle the CEAC organization. Therefore, CEAC continued its work of linking parents and the schools and building bridges of cooperation between the school and the community, one student at a time.

CEAC was founded by concerned African American parents whose children were facing systematic problems with suspension by the school system. In the community of Caucasian parents, there was an organization called "Concerned Parents" that dealt with problems of that population. Each organization functioned independently for the benefit of their children.

However, one afternoon, I received a call from a group of Caucasian parents who were very interested in CEAC. They wanted to join CEAC, dissolve their organization and have one organization to work with parents and children in trouble. This matter was presented to the entire CEAC organization for discussion. The idea of a merger between the two organizations met with lukewarm response. It was temporarily tabled to be again discussed at a later date. I informed the "Concerned Parents" of this postponed decision. By this time, CEAC was past its peak and the merger never occurred.

One particular highlight of CEAC's work in the community was demonstrated at Grice Middle School one morning. The school had invited a touring theatrical group from the Union of South Africa to perform at the school. African American teachers at Grice School were very concerned about the presentations of this group, since the Union of South Africa practiced apartheid, a very oppressive and destructive means of separating the races in that country. The teachers also knew that race relations among students at Grice School were not at all good, and this type of program could reinforce negativity. To that end, the CEAC member of the faculty called Poppy at the Hamilton Neighborhood Service Center, and urged him to get in contact with me, immediately. Poppy agreed to do this. As a result of our conversation, we mobilized about 25 African-American parents and senior citizens to come to Grice Middle School to enjoy the program. I was accompanied by my good friend Dr. David Fluck, a well known figure who was a New Jersey State Medical Examiner.

The school principal called the Superintendent of Schools and he and the Assistant Superintendent in Charge of Curriculum and Staff Development traveled to the school at once.

I was called into the principal's office for a conference with these top officials. Dr. Fluck offered to accompany me. He was initially denied the opportunity on the premise he did not live in Hamilton Township and paid no taxes to support the school. Dr. Fluck informed the administrators that he paid plenty of state taxes and federal, which were distributed to school systems throughout the state, some of which were used for education. He further stated that his friends at Princeton University would enjoy accompanying the "Sixty Minutes" television program on a tour of this school system. That sufficed to open doors.

Our initial meeting with school officials led to subsequent meetings regarding curriculum and staff development for the school system. The Superintendent in Charge of Curricular Revision and Staff Development requested a meeting with a special CEAC committee to discuss curriculum revision, relevant programs and specific training of identified staff members.

For a period of twenty years, 1970-1990, the power and influence of CEAC was felt in the school, in the home, and in the community, including the African American community, of Hamilton Township.

It was an excellent example of how parents, when united, can bring about change in a large school system.

A Heinous Crime Next Door

My daughters and I lived in an apartment complex off Arena Drive in Hamilton Township, New Jersey. Across the street from us was another apartment complex: the Wingate Apartments. These two apartment complexes were often confused with each other because of their proximity to one another.

Right across the street from each other were two apartments; one in each of the different complexes. While I lived in one, two families who later became very good friends of mine, lived in the other. This writing concerns one of those family friends, Mr. and Mrs. Beresford, both Caucasian.

Mr. Beresford was a kind man; his wife was just as kind. Jack Beresford was of advanced age when I first met him; probably in his late 70's. He was already retired from the Department of Corrections, where he was a policeman for many years. In his volunteer service to his community, he often wore his police uniform.

One summer, while I was vacationing with my children in North Carolina, Jack Beresford was stricken with a stroke. It was debilitating and he was unable to recover from it. He died in his early eighties.

Marie Beresford, a slightly built woman, was probably two or three years younger than her husband. I only saw her occasionally, usually when she was working in her flower garden or going in and out of her home from shopping and the like. We spoke to each other and talked briefly about the children. My schedule was a very busy one. I had a full-time position at the College of New Jersey, and a second job working with the Trenton Public School System. That meant I spent little time chatting with neighbors.

After the death of her husband Jack, Marie Beresford kept her apartment and lived alone. On one occasion, she told me that her grown children were unhappy about her living alone. They were trying to persuade her to move in with one of them, or move near them in the Commonwealth of Massachusetts. She was definitely against moving. She felt that she was capable of taking care of herself.

I arrived home about 12:30 p.m. one afternoon from the college, to pick up some items before going out to supervise students in the Pennsbury School District in Pennsylvania. When I turned into the street that separates the two apartments, I was stopped by a police car. He wanted to question me, as well as prohibit me from entering that street. I explained who I was, and gave him my credentials to support my information. Meanwhile, I noticed that many extensive lines of yellow police barricades began at Grady Avenue and Tennyson Drive, and extended as far as I could see at that time.

In dismay and concern, I asked him what had happened and why were there so many police cars, policemen and onlookers. He told me that there had been a murder next door, and that an investigation conducted by the police was underway. "Who?" I uttered in shock.

When I was told that the elderly lady who lived downstairs was found dead by her next-door neighbors, I nearly fainted. However, the policeman moved the barricade and allowed me to enter the street and go home

Subsequently, I was able to put together bits and pieces of information until I saw a total picture of what happened to Marie Beresford that weekend.

Some young men who lived in an adjoining neighborhood knew she lived alone. She also received the daily paper, and it is believed that the paperboy was probably the source of inside information about Marie.

A twenty-five year old "paperboy" came to her home to collect payment either on Friday evening or Saturday morning. She opened the door and allowed him to enter. Her nightmare then began. He robbed her and finally killed her.

By Monday morning, the next-door neighbor had become curious about Mrs. Beresford. They had not seen her during the entire weekend. The weekend papers had gathered at her door and her car had not been moved. Josey, the next-door neighbor agreed with her husband, John, to ring her doorbell and find out if there were any problems.

They rang the doorbell. There was no answer. They rang again. Then they contacted the manager of the complex and reported their concern. He came over and with his key, entered her apartment. There they found Marie Beresford, dead on her bed.

The robber, this paperboy who was eventually convicted, followed this routine: He asked her about her money and jewels; then tore up the house looking for them when what he found was not enough. Then, forced her to get on the bed, where he tied each foot to the two bedposts at the foot of the bed, then tied each of her hands to the head post. She was on her back in the center of her bed, with her legs pulled apart and her arms stretched open. She was scarcely dressed with no undergarments at all. There was evidence of rape, as well as beatings because of the bruises on her body. After inflicting this ordeal on the frail woman, he locked the door and left. I was unable to get information as to the day and time of death. What is known: This woman, who was about 75 years of age, had a weekend of pain, torture and finally, death.

Elsie M. Collins, Ph.D.

Judge Not

Dorothy (pseudonym) was a frail, petite Caucasian lady of considerable age who lived alone. Nobody seemed to visit with her to chat and to pass the time, including her grown grandchildren. There were seven of them; each of her two daughters had children. But, perhaps those young adults were never taught to love and respect their grandmother. Or, perhaps it did not occur to them to visit and look after her for some other reason.

When I first met Dorothy, she was an active business woman representing the firm that employed her with competency and vigor. She was responsible for the implementation and management of the business once the institution had extended the invitation.

Dorothy's business skills were sharp, but so was her tongue. She spoke quickly and only once. For some reason, it seemed to have irritated her if she were asked to repeat a statement or explain again what she meant. She was quick to respond, "Are you deaf?" or "How many times do I have to explain the same information to you?"

I remained friendly with Dorothy, in spite of her steely attitude and blunt responses. As we remained friends over a period of many years, I came to realize that under that hard shell, was a warm, humane person. She was both sensitive and understanding. However, somewhere along life's highway, she had forgotten how to express these attributes to others, and was therefore judged by her peers to be without them.

It was one of the daughters who considered herself "well-to-do, upper-middle class" who severed Dorothy's relationship with her entire family. The daughter, with her husband and children, lived in the Hamilton area section of Trenton and Hamilton. Their white collar "class" propelled them to a sense of superiority they expressed to Dorothy.

Dorothy called me one evening to ask a favor. She asked me to drop her off at Helene Fuld Hospital the following morning on my way to work at the College of New Jersey. She told me that it did not matter how early I went, she would be ready. She said she planned to spend the entire day with her daughter who was in the hospital. Later on, she would be ready for me to pick her up after 7:00 p.m. when I would return home from teaching my graduate class at the college. I agreed to this favor.

Her daughter was seriously ill, and Dorothy knew it. For some reason, she felt the need to spend this particular day, all day, with her. It was a good thing, for the daughter died during Dorothy's visit.

About two years later, Dorothy's younger daughter became seriously ill with a similar stomach condition. Reluctantly, she informed Dorothy of her illness after she was confined to St. Francis Hospital in Trenton. Dorothy spent a great deal of time at the bedside of this gravely ill daughter. After what seemed a brief illness, her youngest daughter also died.

Dorothy had some very serious health problems of her own. Rheumatoid arthritis had left her back curved permanently. She was unable to stand straight, and therefore resembled the shape of a number seven. Both her legs, from her ankle to her knees, were covered with bale-like sores. These legs needed careful and special medical treatment daily. For whatever reason, no medical team came daily, nor weekly to aid Dorothy. She took care of this condition herself. To add to this overwhelming responsibility, was the colonectomy Dorothy had had a few years earlier when the doctors deemed it necessary. Dorothy had to empty the bag and keep the wound clean daily.

My heart went out to Dorothy, for she needed help. I made it my business to do major shopping for her approximately twice a month, and to take her to special appointments and meetings, as the need arose. Dorothy needed only to call, make her request and I was there to help. There were times when my daughter Kimberly helped out Dorothy because I was unavailable.

On one occasion, I did Dorothy's shopping after returning home from church. At this time, I happened to be wearing my floor-length mink coat. After completing my shopping, I lined up with the others at the checkout counter. With her food stamp book in hand, I proceeded to pay for the cart full of food. It was then that the comments, insults and yells began. It took a bit of time before I realized that all attention was focused on me.

When the white (Caucasian) cashier who knew me well realized what was happening, and that these insulting remarks were leveled against me, she came to my rescue. She recognized me to be the lady who took care of shopping and transportation for Dorothy. Immediately, she explained who I was: a Good Samaritan shopping for a "very needy old white lady." Several embarrassed apologies were offered.

While I was away in the South one spring, Social Services moved Dorothy out of her apartment to the Mercer County Geriatric Hospital. This seemed to be the best place for Dorothy to be at this time in her life. I guess she also felt it was time for her to let Social Services take care of her. I continued to keep in contact with her and visited her occasionally, gave her money whether or not she needed it, and called the nursing station in the hospital regularly to check on her.

It was the summer of 1997 or 1998, when I returned to Trenton. I called the hospital to check on Dorothy. The Chief Administrator was unable to find Dorothy's card in the register. That's when I was told that Dorothy had passed away. I was upset and especially saddened, because my very special friend had passed away and I was not there to say goodbye.

Scott Learns Tolerance

Scott (pseudonym), in the mid 1980's, was now a senior in the School of Education at the College of New Jersey. He wanted to be a social studies teacher, and probably one day teach at the school in South Jersey where he got all of his public education.

The all-white, rural, blue-collar culture of students at Camden County High School did not tolerate the presence of non-white students at the school. The few, who attempted to attend the school over the years, were unable to remain and were soon transferred to other schools.

Scott, who was Caucasian, wanted to do his student teaching at Camden County High, but he knew that his faculty supervisor, Dr. Elsie M. Collins, was black. He was afraid that she would be insulted and mistreated when she came for visitation, so he decided to tell her about the negative racial climate that existed within the school.

When I learned of this problem, Scott and I worked out a strategy to combat racist slurs or statements and conduct. When I entered the school, I was prepared for what I faced – coldness, whispers, the use of the word "nigger," stares, laughter, etc., but Scott and I prevailed. Scott also learned. He saw my reaction to this negative climate: patience, understanding and tolerance. He was sympathetic to my situation and ashamed about how poorly I was treated by other whites.

Tileashia

A friend and fellow church member, Mrs. Marie Carroll, a first grade teacher at Parker Elementary School in South Trenton, told me about Tileashia (pseudonym). Tileashia was a little African-American girl in her class with great potential. The girl was smart, alert, and assertive, but her family situation was so poor that there was no motivation available at home. Mrs. Carroll and I came up with a plan that we thought would be beneficial to the youngster. The youngster's mother also agreed and cooperated fully. This was the plan.

Each Sunday morning, I, with my two daughters, would pick the youngster up and take her to Sunday school at St. Paul's. The Sunday school, a supervised teacher-learning program during church service, was well planned at St. Paul's. This youngster would benefit tremendously and enjoy herself. Mrs. Carroll prepared the child and the parent mentally as well as emotionally for the weekend experience. As Tileashia grew older she enjoyed a full day with my daughters and me. This remained intact for the next four years. To date, Tileashia, a young lady, keeps in contact with us.

The More the Merrier

I also made it possible for other children in the City of Trenton to enjoy the children's religious programs at St. Paul's United Methodist Church. The Kelly (pseudonym) children, who were African-American, lived in downtown Trenton. There were three of them, and they were about the same age as my daughters. Their names were Alberta, Mickey and Charles. After discussing the idea with their mother, I agreed to pick up the children each Sunday morning and bring them to church. These children soon became participating members of St. Paul's and even walked to church when I could not pick them up. This relationship with the church continued for at least five years

Doing What You Can to Help

One day, in one of the schools in Burlington County, New Jersey, where I was overseeing student teachers, both the principal and the vice principal contacted me and encouraged me to meet with them in their office as soon as possible. My schedule was quite heavy, but the urgency in their voices moved me to respond right away.

It was early in the month of May, student teaching assignments and responsibilities would soon be over and I was busy completing my responsibilities as Supervisor of my students at this school before returning to The College of New Jersey.

The principal began the conversation by explaining that a dilemma existed and they wished to correct it before more damage could be done. In order to rid themselves of an extremely racist teacher from their faculty, they let her go but wrote her a flowery recommendation which she could use to get into any school system. In their conference with me, they learned that she was applying to be an English teacher in the Trenton Public School System and that her desire was to teach English in Trenton Central High School. The principal and vice principal were very concerned about it because Trenton schools are predominantly black. They knew that a white racist teacher who hated black children would ruin the lives of many for several years. These administrators discussed the situation with me and wanted to know just how well I knew the principal of Trenton Central High School, as well as any board members. I knew the woman who was principal of Trenton Central High. She was a Sorority sister, and I felt I would be able to talk to her on an honest and confidential level. I made a promise that I would do what I could without jeopardizing the integrity of anyone.

When I learned that an English Teacher was being considered for the high school, I went to confer with the principal. I was very frank and honest and spoke candidly about this candidate. The principal of Trenton Central High listened, but soon became very defensive. She did not feel it necessary to contact the administrators of the middle school in Burlington County for further discussion, but chose to hire this teacher. I informed the administrators in Burlington County of my interaction with the principal at Trenton High. The book was closed. The "crusaders" had done all they could.

The Kindness of a Stranger

I was somewhere in Bucks County, Pennsylvania, on my way to observe one of my students who was scheduled to teach in the early afternoon. Since that student's class would occur after the lunch period at school,

I thought it would be to my advantage to have my lunch at one of the fast food shops before I reached the school.

At last, I found one, so I drove into the parking lot and parked the car. When I got inside the restaurant, I joined a long line of individuals waiting to be served. Finally, I reached the counter after a long wait, inching my way forward to touch the serving counter. I had just opened my mouth to make my request to the girl waitress, when she requested loud and clear, looking up at the face of a tall, handsome, white male right behind me, "Can I help you?" He looked down at her calmly, nodded in my direction, and spoke in a loud, clear voice. "Don't you see this lady standing in front of me? Why are you looking in my face?" His response shocked the waitress into reality and created a silence in the listening audience. I was then served with the greatest of respect because of this random gesture of kindness.

The Face of Greed

Anna and Herm Fossenberg (pseudonyms) were a quiet couple who stayed much to themselves. They recently moved to Hamilton Township, New Jersey, where they planned a quiet life of retirement.

Herman worked in middle management for a large corporation in North Jersey. Anna worked in Health Services in the City of New York. Both their children, a son and a daughter, were college graduates and each comfortably established in growing businesses in the Midwest.

The Fossenbergs had lived in their neat, quaint upper middle-class neighborhood for about five years before trouble started. And trouble did start - the most insidious.

The Fossenbergs were of the Jewish faith, but their religious belief was not the problem that gave rise to the trouble. There were several young Jewish families living in the area and none of them had been attacked.

Living in this neighborhood were several families with several children. Most of the children were school-age children in school every day.

There were also school-age children in this neighborhood that did not go to school regularly. These children were considered truants and presented serious problems to the schools. These troubled youth were between the ages of thirteen and eighteen.

Also living in this neighborhood were other troublemakers. They were young adults and/or youth ranging in age from nineteen through twenty-five. It was later discovered that four of these young men had rented a home in the neighborhood and lived there permanently. Their home became a hangout for the teenagers of the neighborhood.

This quiet, well-kept home of young men was, in fact, a house for criminals. The young men dwelling there planned and schemed unlawful conduct to perpetrate against any human target but especially senior citizens.

The neighborhood suspected that this group of young men was involved in some sort of unlawful activities, but there was no proof. Therefore, no charges of any sort could be brought against them.

The Fossenbergs were prime targets. They lived alone, lived an upper-middle-class lifestyle, were well-to-do, and were senior citizens. They were intimidated and threatened constantly.

And so, these young men took advantage of them and caused their lives to be miserable. Fearing for their lives and safety, the couple stayed all day, every day, away from home. Each morning after breakfast, they dressed in some of their finest clothes, put on all of their expensive jewelry, and if it were cold enough, she wore her mink coat. They would take their valuables with them in a bag.

The Fossenbergs went to their favorite shopping center in Ewing, where the Horn & Hardart cafeteria was, and spent the day there. When they returned home, it was usually light enough for the neighbors to see them go inside. What they found numerous times, was a ransacked house. The young men entered their home in search of jewelry, money or any valuables and ransacked their home routinely.

One day while taking a break from my supervisory responsibilities at Ewing High School, I went into the Horn & Hardart cafeteria for lunch and met the Fossenbergs. Many times before I had seen the couple, but never had the opportunity to chat with them. On this occasion I did.

It was clear that the Fossenbergs felt comfortable chatting with me, for soon the conversation became quite serious.

They wanted to tell their story, and so they did. I advised them to go straight to police headquarters right away. I gave them my telephone number with suggestion to call me if needed.

The police became involved, surveillance was put into effect, and after a period of two or three months, the perpetrators were captured, found guilty, and sentenced.

Dr. John Gindhardt

When I first met Dr. John Gindhardt, a Caucasian, I was in my mid-fifties, and he was about 73. He was a tall, handsome man with a head full of mixed gray hair, a deep, rich clear voice, and standing six-feet, three inches tall. When he entered a room he was easily noticed, for his stature commanded attention. Dr. Gindhardt had one problem, however, a very serious one. He was totally blind.

He and his brother Floyd, were among Trenton's prominent medical doctors in mid-twentieth century. His brother was a dentist, and John was a gynecologist. Their offices were located on Hamilton Avenue in Trenton, New Jersey.

However, as their practices grew and expanded, they constructed a building large enough to handle the medical practices of both brothers. It became kind of a medical center on Hamilton Avenue in Trenton.

These young men were the brothers to a very famous New Jersey millionairesse. Her name was Mary Roebling, the heir to the Roebling Steel fortune. It was the Roeblings who gave to the world cables, and these cables made it possible for the United States to move ahead in the building of bridges. The very famous Brooklyn Bridge of New York City was built by the Roeblings. "What Trenton Makes, the World Takes" was a famous slogan that advertised Trenton's very busy iron, steel and cable factories. This was the Roebling family business.

My dear friend, Dr. David Fluck, called me and suggested that I have dinner at his home that particular afternoon. He said that he had something very important to discuss with me, and that he wanted me to give the matter a great deal of thought. Because of a prior engagement I had and would not be home until late, I decided to drive myself to Dr. Fluck's home rather than have him pick me up there.

When I arrived just a bit late, I found Dr. Fluck still quite busy getting things done. Dinner was almost completed. The table was set and the candles were burning low. By the time I hung up my coat, washed my hands and sat down, dinner was served. After grace, Doc

(Dr. Fluck) began to tell me what was on his mind. This is what he wanted me to do.

He asked me to use my influence with the Trenton Rescue Mission to help to make Dr. Gindhardt a member of its board of directors. I was already a member of the board and in a position to influence other members to vote him in as a full member. Secondly, Dr. Fluck asked me to look after Dr. Gindhardt during the meetings, at board functions, and to bring him home following these occasions. Dr. Fluck said that he himself would see to it that Dr. Gindhardt got to the board meetings, and that should not be my concern. But I would have to bring him home.

I took the idea home with me and gave it a great deal of thought. One evening was enough time to give to this request. My answer was yes. I would be delighted to do what I could to help Dr. Gindhardt.

I presented his name to the Board of Directors, with all the necessary credentials required, and he was unanimously voted on the board. Thereafter, Dr. Gindhardt was my date, and I was his, to all functions sponsored by the Rescue Mission Board of Directors.

At the board's annual Christmas dinner celebrations, I ordered his food, cut it up so that he found it in an orderly manner on his plate. Usually wine or stronger alcoholic drinks were available. I made sure his requests were honored.

There were times when we attended other special board-sponsored programs, such as auctions, musical programs, games, etc. Most of the time, for these types of afternoon or evening programs, I picked him up and brought him home.

The Gindhardt/Roebling family kept permanent seats at the Trenton War Memorial Building Patriot's Theater. I was given the privilege of using any one of the vacant seats at any time I chose. On several occasions, I did occupy a seat. There were two occasions when Dr. Gindhardt and I attended a presentation and heard the symphony together.

Dr. Gindhardt lived in the same apartment building – 777 West State Street, Trenton – where his sister, Mary Roebling lived, but he did not live with her. He had his own apartment. Each time I came to pick him up or bring him home, Mary Roebling brought him to the car, helped him get adjusted or helped him out of the car and took him upstairs to his apartment. She did not have her help or the doorman do this for her brother, she did it herself. To expedite comfortably my role in her brother's life, she and I became acquaintances.

On one occasion, Dr. Fluck informed me that Dr. Gindhardt wanted to join our church, St. Paul United Methodist. He told me when this was going to occur and felt that both he and I should sit with Dr. Gindhardt during the services and also accompany him to the altar for the ceremony. I thought a long time about my involvement in this matter but decided that I would sit with these two men during church services, but would not participate in the Baptismal Ceremony. Dr. Gindhardt left the Episcopal Church that Sunday morning and became a United Methodist Church member. Dr. Fluck stood with him.

Once in a while, Dr. Gindhardt would call me at night, sometimes as late as 10:00 p.m. just to chat. It was during these late chats that I learned so much about him.

I learned that he lost his eyesight as the result of an eye operation, performed in Washington, D.C. He felt that there was some negligence involved, but could not prove it. He was into his second marriage and his wife and young twenty-one year old son were on their ranch in West Virginia. They owned a 600-acre ranch in Bluegrass Country in the Shenandoah Valley, West Virginia, and were raising thoroughbred horses.

Dr. Gindhardt eventually became quite ill. In a telephone conversation one night, he explained to me the nature of his illness. He told me that the doctors had discovered a spot on one of his lungs, and they wanted to operate on him to remove that lung. They did, and the operation was a success. Both his wife and young son flew in from the Shenandoah Valley to be with him while he recuperated.

Shortly thereafter, however, the doctors found a lump or growth on the other lung. It was inoperable. His condition worsened and after a few months of illness, he passed away.

I was not paid for my services to Dr. John Gindhardt, and I did not request any payment. Being his friend/date was a lot of fun for me and I began to feel a kinship to him. I was needed by him and became his eyes and his social companion. I felt good about this service to my fellow man. Mrs. Roebling made substantial and consistent donations to the Rescue Mission through me. She made it clear that I need only ask her for a donation, and she would be sure to respond. This continued until the death of her brother and then it stopped. Why it stopped is another story to be told at another time.

Big Blabba Mouths

The following episode took place at a special church event where several United Methodist Churches joined together for worship, music and a meal.

Ona and Janet (pseudonyms), two young, Caucasian ladies, were beside themselves with laughter and giggles, as they pulled off their choir robes in the choir room and prepared to join their buddies in the dining area. They saw me in the audience and guessed that I would be attending the luncheon and afternoon services, as well. Now was the time to talk about that Elsie Collins, and so it began.

Soon Ona and Janet joined their friends in the dining area. Eddy and his friends sat at a table adjacent to that occupied by Ona and her friends. Eddy was my long-time, very good friend, and I had gone out of my way many times to be of service to Eddy.

Eddy was an exceptionally large and fat man. Because of his weight, he was unable to get around freely, nor do many things for himself. For example, his home was located in a group of apartments that I had to pass on my way to and from church. On many occasions, Eddy would ask me to pick him up, bring him home or take him to certain places. I was very happy to oblige.

Because Eddy (pseudonym) lived nearer to Pearson Memorial United Methodist Church than he did to St. Paul's United Methodist Church, he eventually moved his membership to Pearson Memorial for the sake of personal convenience. He was unhappy about the move, but knew he had to do so for health reasons, as well. However, he never severed his friendship with the members of St. Paul's.

Back to the luncheon: I left the luncheon pretty early because I had another engagement to attend that evening.

When I got up from my seat and prepared to leave, giggling and laughter began. Ona and Janet began to tell sordid tales about me. Eddy overheard as these two individuals began tearing into my character. Their running theme was that I was a racist and had a deep hatred for white people. They took bits and pieces of my concerns about the cooperative housing complex where I lived, and blew it out of proportion. They described me as an individual that most white people should fear or stay away from.

Eddy tolerated these lies and jokes as long as he could. His anger was mounting to the point that he could no longer contain himself. He interrupted their conversation, stood up, and came closer to their table.

Everyone stopped talking and a hush fell among the women.

He told them that to defame another person's character, by saying such unkind things about them, was an uncharitable thing to do. Eddy stunned them all by his condemnation of such an act. He let them know that he has known me for many years and that over these years we have been and are still good friends. And perhaps their biggest shock came when he informed them that he would be reporting this incident to the United Methodist Church District Superintendent and also to me.

He did just that. First, he told me about the incident and suggested that the District Superintendent should know about it. Also, he felt that the women, Ona and Janet, should be spoken to by this high-level church official about their non-Christian conduct with the hope that it would make a difference in their lives.

Both Eddy and I reported the incident to Dr. Sadio, the District Superintendent. He was appalled, but thanked us for dealing with it in this manner. He assured Eddy and me that he would speak directly to the woman as soon as possible. Identifying them at Pearson Memorial Church in Hamilton, New Jersey, would not be difficult and by having their names, he would be sure to locate them. He did. Ona and Janet were shocked speechless.

I have seen both Ona and Janet several times since this incident, but neither individual has ever mentioned the character attack they made on me.

A Real Black Person

Paula, a social studies major at Trenton State College (now The College of New Jersey), was doing her senior student teaching in a school system not too far from her home. It was located in one of those rural areas of New Jersey, which was rapidly becoming a suburban. Developers were having great success building spacious homes on farms that once grew corn, beans and vegetables. These upscale communities supported a rather exclusive school system, which was very well equipped with all modern conveniences.

The school building, which was located near Route 202, sat back in what was once a large cornfield. Additional buildings that extended the educational programs of the school were a hot house science building as well as a stadium that overlooked a large, versatile playing field. These buildings extended the educational programs of all secondary students because on these several acres of land sat two schools: the middle school and the senior high school. My visit that day was to the middle school.

When I arrived at the school, sixth graders were just completing their lunch periods and some seventh grade classes had begun to enter the dining rooms for lunch. Since my student teacher taught the eighth grade, I realized that I had at least a half hour before my class would begin. Therefore, I had enough time to take care of the necessary administrative business with the school principal and the cooperating teacher. The afternoon class began at 12:45 p.m. I was seated in back of the classroom with the cooperating teacher, as is usually the case. The class instruction went well. The student teacher was well prepared for instruction. Students were involved, cooperative and responsive to the student teacher's questions and information.

However, there was an undercurrent of excitement in the class and especially among the students. I was aware of this excitement and attributed it to a highly motivated class of students.

A little after 3:00 p.m., I had completed my work with my student teacher and cooperating teacher and was now ready to head home. The cooperating teacher walked with me down the many halls in the school building to the door that led to my car. I could not help but notice groups of children at various turns in the halls or behind some doors along the way pushing and shoving each other. About three groups were noticed by me. The children were not disruptive, nor noisy, but seemed more curious and excited. When the cooperating teacher and I reached either the second or third group of children and their teacher standing in the classroom doorway appearing to be peeping from the room, I became curious and turned to my cooperating teacher for some sort of answer or explanation.

The cooperating teacher, filled with embarrassment by this time, explained to me with this information, "Dr. Collins, this is the first time in their lives these children have ever seen a real black person. Please understand and forgive them for their curiosity." I went immediately into an unoccupied classroom where the children had gathered and were peeping. Other children came in and I spent precious time enlightening the clouded minds of these boys and girls.

Surprised for His Own Good

At this point in Craig's life, he could be considered a full-fledged alcoholic. Not a day passed when he did not take a drink. Since he began to drink early in the morning, by twelve noon, alcohol had obviously taken over his system. His eyes were unfocused, his speech slurred, and he could hardly stand or walk without support.

He had been staying with me a little over two years. I took him in for his own safety and well-being. He was literally homeless at this stage of his life. His mother had recently passed away of cancer, much to the surprise of her family and friends. Craig's father suffered two heart attacks and was unable to care for himself. Therefore, his mother and sisters moved Craig's father to Riverside, New Jersey, where they could supervise his care. His brother Wayne was preparing to enter a new phase in his career after having recently received his Ph.D. from Stanford University in California.

Craig, a brilliant young black man, was taking selected courses in electrical engineering at Rutgers, the State University in New Brunswick, New Jersey. However, he was secretly drinking and had become what's commonly called a "closet drunk."

Before Craig's father moved out of the apartment, he had a conversation with me. He told me that he was going to make two additional months' payment on the apartment, which would give his son Craig ample time to find himself an apartment and move into it. He would also leave enough furniture, plus appliances to furnish a small apartment for his son. He wanted me to be aware of the situation and asked me to make myself available in case Craig needed my advice or assistance. I agreed.

After a few days, I went to visit Craig. I asked about his progress in finding an apartment. I found him practically "out of it." He had taken no steps toward self preservation, but had allowed alcohol to take over his affairs. After observing and studying this desperate situation, I took control of the situation and moved Craig into my apartment. It began as a temporary solution, but because of its complexity, it lasted for several years.

Craig's drinking continued. I knew that the best solution to this problem would be to get him into an alcoholic rehabilitation program. So I sought suggestions from one of my colleagues at The College of New Jersey. Professor Hewitt did volunteer work with an alcoholic rehabilitation center in Pennsylvania. He volunteered his services to help Craig, and would get him involved with a support team as early as necessary. I suggested the sooner the better and Dr. Hewitt began the process immediately.

We decided that until Craig was out of my house and in a program, my role in this process should be limited as follows:

1. Do not discuss alcohol-related problems;
2. Do not encourage him to stop drinking;
3. Carry on normal routine at home;
4. Raise no issues that may cause an argument; and
5. Under no circumstance mention the rehabilitation center.

Dr. Hewitt put together a team of three men, each with a specific responsibility in the process. Two men, one of which being Dr. Hewitt, would enter the house and get Craig, and the third man, which was the driver, would wait in the car.

I was asked to leave the house for work early, as it would not be advisable for me to be present when they took Craig. Sometimes these "pick ups" can be quite ugly. I left the door unlocked to provide easy access for Dr. Hewitt and the men.

When the men arrived, Craig was sleeping in his bed. Craig was shocked and surprised to find two full-grown white men in his bedroom waking him up. I was told that when Craig finally understood the mission of these two sober strong men, a struggle occurred both physically and verbally. After a period of this interaction, there was calm and all three men were able to talk rationally. Craig finally understood and accepted what he had to do for himself and got into the car for the trip to the rehabilitation center in Pennsylvania.

I was called when the process was completed, and I scheduled a follow-up meeting with Dr. Hewitt and the rehab team. I was also given a booklet of written instructions I was to follow to aid in Craig's rehabilitation. He would not return home from the alcohol rehab center for thirty days.

Missed Opportunity

On this particular Sunday afternoon while Dr. David Fluck and I ate an early dinner at his home, he told me that he needed my opinion on a very important business matter. He said that the woman who has served as a private and business secretary to Richard Bilotti, chief editor of the Trenton Times newspaper, was retiring after 35 years of service to him. She would be leaving six months hence.

Dr. Fluck, one of Richard Bilotti's closest friends, had suggested to him that his list of applicants should purposefully include an African-American. He further urged Mr. Bilotti to hire a young qualified African-American to the position.

On this Sunday afternoon, Dr. Fluck told me about his strong suggestion to Mr. Bilotti regarding his new business secretary and encouraged me to have a lengthy discussion on the matter with Bilotti, himself. He told me that at various meetings and situations in which he is involved, it had been noted and pointed out that there was a lack of minority presence in leadership positions, with the exception of schools in the City of Trenton. He felt that this was a problem mainly because African-Americans had been denied access to many of the more visible city positions. He told me, therefore, to have an African-American working as the private business secretary of Mr. Bilotti would be a strong positive step forward.

Dr. Fluck and I discussed the matter at length. I was delighted and told Dr. Fluck that I would search diligently for a qualified individual to apply for the position.

I searched, and telephoned and visited many individuals in Greater Trenton in the interest of filling this position. I, too, agreed with Dr. Fluck's assessment which showed a lack of visibility of African-Americans in areas of prominence in Trenton and wanted to recommend to Dr. Fluck a highly competent individual for Mr. Bilotti's office.

One of the major problems I faced, however, was the lack of a firm written job description. There was no description written for the retiring private business secretary. The job and responsibilities had evolved so that the receptionist eventually found herself fully in charge of all office, managerial, business, receptional, and social affairs that pertained to Mr. Bilotti's office management. To get a better understanding, and a clearer picture of her job, I made a visit to the retiring secretary's office where we discussed at length the job responsibilities.

I soon saw the total picture that described the retiring secretary's responsibilities. They were: to carry out all secretarial services; manage/control the scheduling of all meetings and appointments; be available to attend specific meetings as assigned; prepare and submit special reports as needed/required; meet and confer periodically with Mr. Bilotti; keep office area orderly and clean; and be present in the office not less than three working days per week.

With the job description in hand, I again resumed my search for a competent receptionist.

I was unable to find the top-notch competent individual needed to meet these qualifications, but I knew a young lady who had most of the skills. With determination and dedication, she could certainly fulfill this requirement within a few months. So I went to see her.

We talked at length about the job. Jamie was quite interested. The salary was agreed upon, hours were acceptable, and all questions and concerns that Jamie had were adjusted to fit her particular situation. Jamie suggested the day she wished to begin working at her new job, so I left such final agreements between Jamie and Mr. Bilotti.

Two weeks later, I made a follow-up call to Jamie's home to discuss her progress and was very disappointed to hear Jamie's response: "Oh, I didn't go to that job. I was going to tell you, but hadn't gotten to it yet." The women simply did not follow through and take advantage of a great opportunity.

Mr. Richard Bilotti then just did his own recruiting. Two to three weeks later he hired a young woman from Princeton, New Jersey.

18 Months Old – And Then Gone

I was just returning home from The College of New Jersey where I had spent all afternoon writing reports, evaluations and recommendations.

A short distance after turning off Cedar Lane onto Berg Avenue, I had to stop my car right in the middle of the street. I could go no further because a grayish-black car was parked in a position that did not allow enough room for any car to pass it. I also noticed a woman walking around the car as if looking for someone or something, wringing her hands and wiping her brow. She looked distraught.

I got out of my car and walked over to the lady to see if she needed help. The woman continued to walk aimlessly, slightly bent over, while turning her head from left to right, as if looking for something.

I was finally able to get her attention and asked her what was wrong and if she needed assistance. After several attempts to get her attention, she finally responded. However, she mumbled and grumbled incoherently.

Then suddenly a woman burst out of the house on the left-hand side of the street where the two cars were parked. She was screaming the name of a child, "Brady, Brady," she called "Where are you Brady? Come here Brady, come here." At the same time, she began to look behind shrubbery, trees and bushes for this child, Brady. She became more and more desperate as she looked and could not find him. Meanwhile, other members of the family came out of the house and joined the search.

At a distance, near the rear of the house, a voice rang out, "Here he is." She picked up Brady's lifeless body and brought it to the front of the house. The incoherent woman whose car was badly parked in the middle of the street, had hit him and killed him instantly. A chorus of painful screams filled the air. Brady was only 18 months old. Now he had gone to join his mother who was killed a few months earlier on Arena Drive, while backing out into that very busy thoroughfare.

The sudden death of this wee fellow in my neighborhood brought upon me a series of sleepless nights.

A Particular Brand of Spite

I was out looking for another vehicle and decided that I would purchase a new car this time and that it would be a Chrysler.

I went to the Chrysler dealer on Route 33 in Hamilton Township, New Jersey to see if they had anything I liked. But, I would not make any definite decisions before contacting Mr. Harris of White City, a section of Trenton, to accompany me.

I highly respected Mr. Harris, and regarded him as an honest and good man. Over the years since I had owned a car, Mr. Harris had been my mechanic. His regular job was with the Bethlehem Steel mills in Pennsylvania. But he also had worked as an auto mechanic with local businesses, thus using his special training in mechanical engineering while in the service during World War II.

I depended upon Mr. Harris' expert opinion as far as my car was concerned, and I wanted him to be a part of my decision-making process.

I saw the car I liked. It was a four-door Chrysler, eight cylinder, and deep maroon in color. The salesman gave me the typical sales talk about the car, but being a neophyte on this matter, I was unable to internalize the information properly. I would have Mr. Harris to talk directly with the salesman.

Mr. Harris set the date and time when he'd be able to accompany me to the Chrysler dealer and showroom. Since he worked nights, he wanted to set a day when he would be off and able to spend a good deal of quality time with me in the store.

The mission was accomplished after spending a great deal of time with the dealer and others. The dealer explained the payment plan of the company, but also pointed out that I could save $3,000 if I paid cash for the car, rather than accepting the installment plan extending payments to three to five years.

I decided upon the cash payment strategy, but would have to make necessary arrangements to self-finance.

I decided Joey, a friend of the family, would be just the right person to ask about a short term loan. He was financially capable of making such a loan since winning a million dollar law suit against the New York City Board of Education. While exercising at school, Joey in a freakish accident broke his neck and was paralyzed from his neck down, and was unable to care for himself. A specially-equipped room was prepared for him at Allie's and Jimmie's home in Teaneck, New Jersey and an individual was hired to care for him. Joey was almost like a family member, living in my sister's home and being the brother of Toni, one of Allie and Jimmie's foster children.

My daughters and I went to Teaneck to spend the weekend with Allie and Jimmie. Besides enjoying a visit with my sister and family, I wanted to negotiate a loan of almost $15,000 for my new car. This was the mid 1980's.

I presented the request to Joey, a discussion followed, family members were called in, an agreement was reached, and a contract was signed.

The terms of the contract were as follows: to complete the debt of $15,000, I would mail to Joey a check for $300 within the first five days of each month for the next four years and two months. This would total $15,000. As a bonus, I would make a contribution of $150 to Joey for his cooperation.

Joey's lawyer issued to me a cashier's check to cover the full cost of the new Chrysler that I was to purchase. I returned to Hamilton Township and within a few days, Mr. Harris and I went to the Chrysler dealer to purchase my car. The dealer suggested that it would be to my advantage to allow them to service and maintain the car periodically/annually. Since it was a new car, it would not need much to keep it in excellent condition with the proper maintenance service. Along with Mr. Harris, I, too, thought it was a good idea and agreed to allow the Chrysler dealership on Route 33 take over the maintenance of the car.

For the first few years all went well. The car was serviced annually according to its need and requirements. Then, about the third year, problems began to occur. They were not specific problems like the battery, engine, carborator, etc., but a system-type problem. It became more and more difficult to turn over the engine each day. I became quite alarmed. My car was only three years old, I was the only owner, and there was regular maintenance. What could be the problem that could not have been detected during on-going service to the car? Mr. Harris helped find another reputable auto mechanic to do a complete overhaul. I left the car with the mechanic a few days as requested.

This auto mechanic found the problem and sat Mr. Harris and I down to explain it to us.

Iron particles and iron dust were distributed throughout the entire system of the car. They were in the motor, the battery, the carburetor, the transmission, the air conditioning system, etc. The build-up had been continuous over a period of time so that now many major car functions were compromised. The iron particles and dust had jammed or disabled them. We asked how this could happen to a new car, and he assured us such things must have been deliberately done. Someone with access to shaved iron and iron dust continuously poured these particles and dust into sensitive and specific openings and parts of the car until the machinery began to strain. He told me the entire system of the car is poisoned and nothing can be done to heal it.

When the Chrysler dealer and mechanic division were confronted with this problem, and the evidence that led to the problem, they denied any wrongdoing. Naturally, they pointed their fingers to the manufacturer, and promised to contact the company in this regard.

They never did, nor did they take any responsibility for the demise of my four-year old maroon Chrysler. I am afraid that some people, motivated by envy or racism or both did not like the idea of someone like me driving a fine motor car bought with cash.

Special Dates with David Fluck: Wanamaker's

What was it about Wanamaker's that excited so many? I didn't get it. To me, Wanamaker's was just another large department store in Philadelphia where people came to shop. On weekends it was especially crowded. People were home from work and other responsibilities, and could spend more time in downtown Philadelphia, including Wanamaker's.

Periodically, Dr. Fluck would ask, "Do you want to go to Wanamaker's today?" "Don't you think it's about time to go to Wanamaker's?" I didn't immediately get the point about going specifically to Wanamaker's, but I would agree and off we went to Philadelphia.

I grew up in New York City. During my early teen years the family lived in Jamaica, New York, but by the time I was seventeen years old, we had moved to Harlem in uptown Manhattan.

New York City is a "hub" of activity. It is the world's fashion center. Several of the nation's colleges and universities are located in the city, and among many other leading centers, it is also the nation's entertainment center, with the finest plays and shows on Broadway.

I was always surrounded by an element of excitement, and shopping at America's finest stores was a part of that excitement. Saks Fifth Avenue, Lord & Taylor, Russex, Bergdorf Goodman's, and Macy's were top fashion centers located downtown on Madison Avenue and Fifth Avenue, to name a few. I did my exclusive shopping there and I frequented shows, plays and movies on Broadway in the 1950's while completing studies at Columbia University.

But there was something about Wanamaker's that beckoned women and men, young and old, white and black, who lived in its environs and neighboring states. They flocked to Wanamaker's especially on weekends to socialize.

A friend in the Trenton area, Patricia Morelli, told me that when she was a little girl going to Wanamaker's was a very "big deal." Her mother took her to Wanamaker's and met with other friends at designated areas of the store. These friends socialized, ate and shopped in a divine atmosphere that seemed to be designed for their entertainment. This socializing ritual went on every weekend for some time, twice a month for some, and once a month for others. For those like me, going once in a while was quite sufficient.

When Doc and I went to Wanamaker's it was usually an all-day outing. He would pick me up from home around 10:00 Saturday morning; take the hour's ride to Philadelphia to Wanamaker's. Once at Wanamaker's, we would spend the rest of the day. I would visit my favorite departments, located on various floors of the very, very large store. Sometimes Doc would meet me at a special clothing or jewelry department, and I would model some clothing for him. Other times, he would busy himself looking for things. At a designated time, we went to lunch at Wanamaker's swanky restaurant. We would spend the rest of the afternoon eating and chatting. After lunch, Doc would take a long route home. Many times he drove to the King of Prussia shopping center where he pointed out new areas of development. Often he drove by a very upscale housing area in Bucks County where the houses sold for the incredible sum of one million dollars.

Doc and I would reach home in the early evening. Doc would drop me at home, visit and then travel to his home. Since this was on Saturday, I had more time left in the weekend to complete my homework and prepare for next week's lessons. But I was not about to wait until the last minute to do my school work. After a full day of shopping in Philadelphia, I would sit down, get busy and for the next three hours, at least, prepare my school work.

The Experience at Sterling High School

Education majors who were studying to be teachers had two supervisors to observe them at the school where they were doing their student teaching. One supervisor came from the College's School of Liberal Arts and was a representative of the subject area in which the student majored. For example, if the student were an English major an English professor came, and if the student were a history major, a history professor supervised. The other required supervisor came from the School of Education to observe the student's proficiency in the techniques and strategies of teaching. Since these supervisors came from different schools and departments of the college, their schedules rarely, if ever, coincided. This meant that, very rarely, if ever, they met at the same time at a public school to observe a student who was teaching a class on a particular day.

However, this rare meeting did occur at Sterling High School (pseudonym) in central New Jersey one spring morning.

As the education supervisor, I arrived at Sterling High fairly early for the 9:00 a.m. class. My student, Mark Jensen (pseudonym) was to teach. I went straight to the classroom, after finding its location, and took my seat in the back of the room. Almost immediately, Dr. Fred Kelso (pseudonym), supervisor from the History Department came into the classroom. We were both surprised and happy that we had come at the same time to observe.

Mr. Don Braun (pseudonym), with Mark, the college student, came in together just as the students who were to take this class also came in. Mr. Braun was the cooperating teacher.

This was a class of eleventh graders, so that it didn't take them long to file in the classroom, find their seats, and get quiet. Almost immediately, they got out their books, notebooks and pads, maps and whatever else was necessary to prepare for this class in American history they were about to take.

It was obvious at this point, that Mark, the student teacher, was not demonstrating strength and leadership skills necessary to command control of this class, and maintain their interest. He seemed to be aimless as he went to the seats of a couple of male students in front rows and whispered something to them. A few minutes had passed and the class of about twenty-two students was beginning to get restless and talkative.

Finally, Mark raised his voice and began to open class. The first complete statement to come out of his mouth was: "We have a nigger in the back of this classroom and we must do something about it." It was obvious that Mark held negative attitudes about black people. He was angry because his supervisor was black – a nigger! That's why he made this racist, and stupid, statement.

At that moment, there was an outburst of laughter by the students and some hand clapping. Dr. Kelso sprung to her feet in anger, made a remark to the student teacher and went straight to the main office.

The cooperating teacher was also shocked and angry, and took control of the classroom. I gathered my belongings and also went to the main office to report this incident.

The school administration tried to play down the incident as a mistake or a slip of the tongue, and that it would not happen again. Both Dr. Kelso and I knew that the ugly remarks made were deliberate and we both thought the school and the student should be held responsible.

They were. The College discontinued its relationship with Sterling High School and discontinued the cooperating experience for a period of five years. Also, the College requested two letters of apology: one was sent to me and one was sent to the college.

Interesting Experiences and People in the State of North Carolina

Miles Past Home

Vacation time was here at last and I was about 19 years of age. Kittrell College was closed for the summer and I was going to Wilson's Mills to spend a few days with my grandmother before going home to New York. I wanted to get home early so I could begin my summer's work and get money for college. I thought it best to go to Wilson's Mills now, while I was already in North Carolina.

I boarded the Southern Passenger Train in Kittrell, North Carolina, which took me to Raleigh. There I would change trains and board the Atlantic Coast Line, which would take me to Wilson's Mills.

My layover in Raleigh was a few hours, so I took a taxi to Aunt Rachel's and Uncle Thomas Hayward's home, where I could relax. Aunt Rachel was my grandmother's sister. Aunt Rachel and Uncle Thomas always had delicious food on hand and I did not hesitate to stay for dinner.

They were long time residents of Raleigh, and were therefore, well established residents of their neighborhood. Even though they had no children, they maintained a fairly large home for two people which became the stop-over place for friends and family members.

Uncle Thomas always kept a watchful eye on the time, to make sure I did not miss my train to Wilson's Mills. When it was time to leave for the train station, he put me in a taxi and sent me on my way.

My train left Raleigh at 10:00 p.m. It was an hour's ride to Wilson's Mills, so I wouldn't arrive until 11:00 p.m. I boarded the train in Raleigh and settled back for my ride.

Jack Jones would meet me at the station and walk me to my grandmother's home. Jack was between 13 and 14 years old. He was one of Miss Stella and Mr. Jesse Jones' younger sons. Since they lived downtown near the railroad station, Jack usually met the train when I visited my grandparents and he'd walk me to their home.

The train whistle blew its familiar melody, announcing its imminent arrival and the waiting crowd began to move out of the depot and take their selected spots along the tracks. Small town, familiar chatting filled the air as the crowd milled about.

The train roared closer and closer, while maintaining its fast deliberate speed. When it reached the Wilson's Mills depot, it continued its journey and made no attempt to stop, nor slow down. The few people who had gathered at the depot to board the train were stunned. But nobody was more surprised than I. Where was this train taking me!

Frantically, I ran to locate the conductor, porter or any train man who could help me. I found someone.

The response was odd. The train finally stopped miles past Wilson's Mills in a place where there was no station. The night was dark; the area was remote and unpopulated. I was assisted in leaving the train, and then the train moved on. I was frightened out of my wits, but had to get to my grandmother's, so I walked. That company should have been sued for its conduct. Had I been white would they have gotten away with that negligence? No!

I was alone and frightened, but I maintained my sense of composure. Holding onto my luggage and my pocketbook, I got in the middle of the railroad tracks and walked the miles back to Wilson's Mills.

Sister Sally

In the northeast section of Wilson's Mills, usually referred to as the "black section" of the small town, Miss Sally lived with her husband, Purl. Miss Sally A. Grady had come to Wilson's Mills from her home and family in Dudley, Wayne County, North Carolina. She was a recent graduate from Shaw University, Raleigh, in the field of Elementary Education, and now she was ready to take her first job as a teacher. And so she had come to Wilson's Mills to join two other women teachers. These women: Lottie Holt, Mamie Grandy, and Sally Grady, were assigned to the Wilson's Mills Elementary School for Colored Students, to teach "colored" youngsters in grades "primer" (kindergarten) through grade eight.

In those years, when unmarried male or female teachers came to a community to work, they had to find a home that would provide for them a room and board. Sally found such a "rooming" place in the home of my grandparents. There she met her future husband, Purl. In 1910 when she was twenty-five and he was twenty-three, they were united in Holy Matrimony.

Sally came from a very large family and from all indications, a very strong family heritage. Her father, Thomas Grady, an ex-slave, was a very dark-skinned and well-built man. Legend has it that he was considered handsome, also. Over his lifetime, Thomas had two wives and thus two sets of children, which totaled 16 children in all. His first wife was a blond haired, blue-eyed Mulatto woman whose name was Smithy Cobb. They had twelve children. Sally was a member of this group and she was child number six. Her brothers and sisters were Joseph, Mary, Leala, Walter, James, William, Clifford, Rena, Hugh, Connor, and Timothy.

After several years of marriage, Smithy passed away, and at the appropriate time, Thomas Grady married a woman named Lu Karnega, a Native American. Of this union, four children were born: Minnie, Nathaniel, John and Luetta.

The Civil War ended in 1865. For the next 35 years, until 1900, Americans were busy "binding up the nation's wounds." This period of time in the nation's history is known as "Reconstruction." During this time, Thomas Grady, uneducated, became what may be considered a fairly well-to-do gentleman. He accumulated hundreds of acres of land and became a successful family motivator and encouraged each child to either become a professional by attending college, or become proficient in a trade or occupation. All of them took their father's advice and became successful and productive citizens, except two: one who died in infancy, and Leala, who was hit by a car and who later was sent to a mental institution.

At the time of his death, Thomas Grady owned a great deal of property in Wayne County. Therefore, in his Will, he made sure that each child received a fair amount of the land and property that he owned. This inheritance was quite beneficial for it enabled the farming children, as well as the business traders, to build profitable businesses.

When Lu Karnega passed away, she left four very young children. Luetta, the youngest of them was almost three years old. When a situation like this occurred in the black population, it was the custom to divide the children up and send them to live with relatives to be raised. All four children were sent to live with older siblings, and Luetta was sent to live with her sister Sally and husband Purl (my aunt and uncle), in Wilson's Mills.

Sis Sally was a married woman now, and her husband was Dominion Purl Richardson, affectionately called D.P.

My grandfather's one-and-a-half acre lot of land provided enough space for a second house to be built next door to his home. So my grandparents deeded to Purl and Sally enough land for them to build themselves a very comfortable home. Over the years, Purl and Sally's home became one of the more fancy homes in town. It eventually had six rooms, plus a long hall that began at the front door and ran the length of the house. At the end of the hall was an enclosed back porch from which one could enter the kitchen, the long hall, a large bathroom, and back steps to a large back yard. The backyard extended the entire length of his father's back yard and each was large enough to accommodate a fairly large vegetable garden. Every year, both Purl and his parents had beautiful vegetable gardens.

In the 1920's, funds from the Rosenwald Foundation were made available to build schools for "colored" children. One was built in Wilson's Mills, and it replaced the wooden three-room school where Sis Sally worked. The school's four teachers were sent to different schools to work. Sis Sally was sent to an elementary school across the Neuse River in a small town called Red Hill. This too, was a Rosenwald School and Sis Sally became the head teacher and was later known as a teaching principal. This was in the 1940's. Sis Sally's teaching career lasted fifty years. Upon retirement she was honored at a special celebration by her colleagues and the County Superintendent of Schools.

College Racists – On the Train

I had enjoyed my week-long stay at Spelman College in Atlanta, Georgia. Now it was time to go home to Dover, and I was ready for that, too.

Alpha Kappa Alpha Sorority held a very important Regional Conference, the Boulet, at Spelman in Atlanta. I was sent as a delegate representing my chapter, Epsilon Iota Omega, of Delaware State College.

Now, the week to ten days of meetings, conferences, caucuses, chats, brainstorming, planning, decision-making, voting, greetings, etc., were over and delegates were on their way home.

Unlike many of my sorors, I went to Atlanta by train, while many others went by air or car. With the delegate money given to me by my chapter, I purchased a round-trip, first-class accommodation from Wilmington, Delaware to Atlanta, Georgia.

The conference was held in the month of May. The countryside was in bloom with an array of colors everywhere. Wonderful scents, and odors filled the air and combined with sounds of pleasure so that the warm breezes seemed to envelop everyone, everywhere. Like others, I was enjoying the evening's breezes and scents, while I waited for the train at the small station in Atlanta.

The year was 1957. This meant that the state and national laws enforcing segregation of races and discriminatory practices against non-whites were in place. Signs that read "white" and "colored" were boldly placed in the appropriate places in Atlanta. They were also displayed in places such as the station's waiting rooms, water fountains, train ticket window and public restrooms. Although I had lived for many years in New York City with my parents, I was born in Durham, North Carolina and spent my early years in the South living with my grandparents. So I knew and understood the laws enforcing segregation and discrimination, and obeyed them.

Also waiting for the train were several young white males, students from a nearby college. There were approximately eight to ten of them. It was obvious that they were in a festive mood. Their voices were loud, boisterous, filled with laughter and fun, and occasionally augmented with profanity. It was also quite clear that some of them had consumed quite a bit of alcohol. Probably the effects of the alcohol had pushed them into a level of arrogance and hostility.

Train officials knew that students from this college seriously objected to African Americans riding in the first-class section of the train with them. And in the past, problems had developed because of it. Therefore, on this beautiful spring evening, it was quite possible, given the emotional and physical condition of those young men, that problems could develop.

Fagen, an African American man, had a few vacation days left, so he had come to Atlanta to spend time with his parents. Now, he was on his way back home to Philadelphia. Fagen, the younger of two sons, was from a family of educators. He was a graduate of Morehouse College in Atlanta and was planning to pursue a master's program at Temple University in Philadelphia. He worked for the federal government in the area of Secret Service and was not at liberty to explain to me the nature of his job responsibilities. He was, however, fully armed.

The nature of his job responsibilities kept him on the alert which meant that he was able to sense trouble brewing long before it actually occurred. On this occasion, he knew trouble was around the corner.

He made friends with me. In his easygoing soft spoken manner, one would never know that he was an undercover agent, well-equipped with special top-level training and active firearms.

We talked about topics that were familiar, such as education, family, the weather, etc. During our chats, he informed me that he had moved his compartment/room on the train directly across the aisle from mine for security reasons. He also went into some detail about the possible racist riot that was being planned by the students from the college. He explained that some troublemakers were already on the train, and others would be getting on at certain given stations. He stated that train officials were already alerted and he had joined the security network that was being organized.

When the train arrived, Fagen, along with the train conductor, escorted me to a particular compartment in a secured area. Just as he had promised, Fagen was nearby. I was given the following instructions: do not respond to noises in the halls; do not open your door; do not leave your compartment alone; do not talk to anyone; and do not answer anyone. I was given specific codes and answers to use in response.

There was upheaval and loud noise throughout the night. I did not leave my room at all, and followed, very carefully, all instructions that had been given to me. My food was sent to me from the dining car and Fagen visited me about three times to make sure I was safe. I could barely sleep that night, not only because of the noise in the area, but also because of the threats and name-calling. "Nigger, we know where you are. You had better beware." The word "nigger" became their theme all night long. I was terrified.

When dawn came, there was calmness as the train continued to slice its way northward. It was speculated that one or all of these three situations occurred: 1) some of the troublemakers had gotten off the train at an appointed destination; 2) some of them had been arrested and/or detained by authorities; and 3) others were asleep in their compartments.

About 9:00 a.m., I responded to Fagen's coded knock at my door and joined him at breakfast in the dining car. I was greeted by train officials who extended their apologies for the disturbances of the night and assured me that I was safe. Fagen and I then exchanged credentials and decided to cultivate our friendship. We remained very good friends until Fagen's untimely death in the early 1980's.

John Charles Clark

John Charles and I loved, honored and respected each other, just as cousins should. Once a year, when I visited Wilson's Mills during the Son's and Daughter's Homecoming in October, we had fun eating, dancing and even drinking a little moonshine whiskey. I do not like moonshine, but pretended to drink some when John Charles offered it to me. I had, over the years, developed a tactful method of getting rid of it, by pouring the liquor in other nearby cups or glasses or on the ground, when the opportunity presented itself. So, naturally, I employed this strategy with John Charles.

Unfortunately, John Charles had become an alcoholic by this time (his early forties), and took every opportunity to partake of all the drinks placed before him.

Watching my handsome cousin drink away his life in such a manner concerned me a great deal, and I had to find out what happened in his early life that brought him to this state. What I learned is that John Charles was the victim of a barrage of racist attacks upon his mind and spirit, something that eventually destroyed him.

John Charles was one of seven children, born to Naomi and Hubert Clark. He was the third child, after his sister, Ora Lee, and his brother, Hubert, Jr. His grandmother, Florence Richardson, was considered a full-blooded Native American and his grandfather, John Richardson, was the brother to my grandfather, Emzy Richardson.

All of the Clark children were considered gifted and academically smart, and all of them went on to achieve business and/or academic goals. In the mid-twentieth century, a very large percentage of the African Americans were living below the poverty line. Expensive educational opportunities were out of their reach, mainly because of segregation and discrimination, and secondly because of lack of funds.

Civil rights legislation opened many doors for them, and with the help of the school and teachers, the Clark children entered the right doors and received an excellent education. All seven of these children seized the opportunities:

- Ora Lee became a beautician and eventually opened her own shop in Clayton, North Carolina;
- Hubert opened his own barber shop with eventually four chairs in Durham, North Carolina;
- John Charles received a BA degree, graduated from Kent College (now Kent State University) in Ohio, and earned a MA degree in Education Administration from the University of Oklahoma;
- Ruth received a BA degree in Language Education from Kent College. She was able to speak fluently in four languages: Russian, German, French and Spanish. She also had command of root language of Latin. She enrolled at Shaw University to pursue a master's degree in Language;
- George (G.W.) was a graduate of Kent, earned a master's degree at Iowa State University, and completed doctoral work at the University of Chicago. He later joined the

faculty of Iowa State University, where he taught Political Science;

- Eliza earned a BA degree at Kent, and a MA at New York University. She became a teacher supervisor in the New York City school system;
- Esther earned her BA degree from City College, New York and her master's degree at New York University. She taught elementary school in the New York City school system

John Charles was a physical education and science teacher at schools in Wake County before he took, with great delight, the honorable job of principal of the African American High School in Henderson, North Carolina.

Segregated schools were mandated throughout the South at that time. On the other side of town from African American High School, across the railroad tracks, was the "White school." Each of these schools was in a separate, independent part of town. Each had its own hierarchy and personnel.

John Charles was well equipped with the skills, know-how, and preparation to run a school. His degree in administration had prepared him well.

Among the new personnel he was privileged to hire would be his little sister, Ruth, who was considered a genius in her field of languages. Within a few years after she came on board as a teacher, she set up a Foreign Language Department. Her strategy was to make it possible for each high school student to be exposed to three years of a foreign language and to be able to spend two consecutive years taking one of them. This would give the student an opportunity to both read and speak one foreign language upon graduation from a four-year high school program.

Ruth's strategy worked. It was so successful that it was given the name Ruth's Foreign Language Plan or the Ruth's Plan.

Parents in the Caucasian "white" high school system began to ask questions. They wanted to know why the students in the colored high school were receiving special and advanced courses in foreign language and their children were not. They requested the same kind of foreign language program in their school for their children that the "colored" children were receiving.

The Superintendent of Schools set out to rectify the problem. He required Ruth to duplicate the foreign language schedule in the Caucasian school that she had set up in the colored school. Then he required her to spend two days per week in the Caucasian school teaching foreign languages. She was also required to teach the Caucasian teachers how to supervise and coordinate the language program.

Ruth was now teaching in two separate high schools weekly. Her teaching responsibilities were doubled; the distances she traveled daily were doubled; and the personnel with whom she worked were different. These additional responsibilities began to take a toll. Overwhelmed, she turned to alcohol for relief and comfort.

After three years of working part-time in the African American school as supervisor of the language department, and part-time in the Caucasian school in the same position, Ruth was removed from the African American school to become full-time in the Caucasian school.

Ruth's alcohol dependency gradually increased as she sought comfort from emotional and mental pain.

John Charles was likewise undergoing mental and emotional distress. His academic program was under attack. His foreign language program had been dismantled and he was powerless to stop the destruction. Negotiations, adjustments in salaries, and even threats to report the assault to the State Department of Education made no difference. His voice was completely ignored, even by the State Department, for he later learned that the conduct of Henderson's white Superintendent of Schools was condoned. John Charles also began to turn to alcohol to find relief from the pain of emotional and mental hurt. He, like his sister Ruth, was a closet drinker. Both continued to work at their jobs.

The biggest slap in the face came with the integration of the schools. By the mid 1960's, all segregated schools throughout the nation were mandated by law to integrate. This problem was solved throughout the South by closing the African American schools, and busing these children to the white schools. In 1965, all the African American children were ordered by law to report to the once all-white schools to begin their classes. Elementary, junior high school and senior high school children were affected.

All of the African American teachers were also affected. Teachers in these schools that were either torn down and/or closed were also displaced. The African American teachers and administrators suddenly had no jobs. The Superintendent of Schools, with the Board of Education, set about to find jobs for these individuals whenever there was a vacancy or need. Some of the African American educators were placed in jobs in different school systems, some of them received part-time employment, and others were out of work for years and then finally placed in a school.

With his school now defunct, John Charles was placed in another position, but his new assignment he viewed as demeaning since it did not take advantage of his skills as an educator. He was put in charge of the buses at the high school. He had to make sure that the buses followed their assigned schedules so that the children arrived at school on time, and left school on the correct bus. John Charles' salary was scaled down to match his non-academic work responsibilities.

Ruth was retained at the high school where she was needed to carry on the Foreign Language Program. Her master's degree from Shaw University made her one of the best and only individuals qualified to create and supervise the academic department in foreign languages. Yet the school principal had placed her under the supervision of the white language teacher whom Ruth had taught.

John Charles worried continuously about his little sister and tried, in vain, to get her out of that school system. Meanwhile, his alcohol dependency increased as did his sister Ruth's. They both maintained high profiles, however and were involved in meaningful community affairs.

The African American population of Clayton was pressuring the city government to allocate a selected/secluded area of the town for decent housing for their population. This fight, which had been going on for many years, required constant leadership and pressures on the city officials. John Charles was one of the African American leaders who worked tirelessly on this project. An area called Rolling Woods was finally designated in the 1970's, and John Charles' family, along with one other family, built the first homes in the area. About this time, John's marriage had gotten into serious trouble. Some of the reasons came from his continuous drinking habits; others could be attributed to the emotional problems of worrying about his own financial needs. John's community standing had been lowered. He felt that he no longer made enough money to educate his children, and that he was a failure. His marriage finally ended. John Charles' wife and children moved out of their new home in Rolling Woods. After a short stay in Henderson, North Carolina, she and the children moved back to Oklahoma City, her hometown. She continued her teaching career there.

John Charles and his wife tried to put their marriage back together. After several attempts, they finally agreed that it was too late to mend the damage that had been done. John Charles had become a full-fledged alcoholic, but continued to deny it. This meant that the therapy he needed for rehabilitation was out of the question.

During these turbulent years in the lives of the Clark family, John's father, Hubert, passed away at age 99. His mother, Naomi, who was fifteen years younger than her husband, continued to fight for her children's well-being. Naomi was overcome with grief and pain as a result of the things happening to Ruth and John Charles.

Alcohol finally won its battle with Ruth, and shut down her entire career. She became so ill emotionally and physically, that she was no longer able to live alone. Her beautiful home in Clayton, North Carolina was eventually sold and Ruth was moved back into her mother's home where family members took turns caring for her. Finally, she passed away in the mid 1980's after a very short teaching career of fifteen years.

The end of John Charles' career was also abrupt. After many years of alcohol dependency, his job performance suffered and his health failed. He, too, was forced to resign from his chosen career in education. For many years, he tried to get his mother and sister, Ora Lee, to move out to Rolling Woods and live with him. They would not, but chose to continue to live in their old home in the colored section of the town, Clayton. So John continued to live alone and continued to drink his alcohol. In the late 1980's, he became desperately ill and was rushed to Duke Hospital in Durham. He passed away in 1987, a few years after the death of his sister Ruth. His mother, Naomi, passed away one year later, in 1988.

Interesting Experiences and People in the State of New York

Fear

When I descended the steps of the elevated train, the third different train, including a bus I had taken to get to my school in Sheepshead Bay, I was relieved. The ride was tiresome somewhat, but my anxiety to get to school, meet the administration, and then get to my classroom to meet the students, was a pleasant motivation.

However, I was not prepared for what I met at the bottom of the stairs from the elevated train. It was a crowd and what a crowd! I was startled and taken aback. This line of individuals, which began at the exit gate of the elevated train, ran the entire six blocks and terminated at the school door. The lines formed a corridor, which consisted of mothers, fathers, grandparents, aunts, uncles, other relatives and friends. It consisted of shopkeepers, shop workers, handymen, drivers, managers, owners of shops, CEO's, young children, children who had cut school, babies, and even volunteers.

I looked out at that crowd, the strong manner it had presented itself, and my heart sank. I had no idea just what was in the crowd's mind. And I did not know whether or not harm would come to me from this crowd. But I would not allow fear to overcome me. Armed with my philosophy of positive thinking and steadfast devotion and faith, at

35 years old, I maintained my self-control. With my head held high, I began my march to the school. This five foot, two inch, one hundred ten pound young woman very carefully made her way through a packed human corridor.

The crowd was peaceful. Individuals chattered with each other, whispered with hands to their mouths, made loud condescending remarks and occasionally someone was insulting or threatening. But no one touched me, nor threw objects at me.

The six blocks I had to walk seemed like miles to me. There were times along the journey, when my heart leaped with fear. I was not quite sure whether or not some one would hit me, knock me down or harm me in other ways. I chewed up my fear, spit it out, and kept my cool and marched on.

Finally, after walking for what seemed an eternity, I reached the school. What a relief!

However, what awaited me inside was a bombshell – sitting, standing, strolling about and yelling at each other was a classroom of 20-30 unruly, ninth grade, Hasidic Jewish girls. They were ready for me, and had already made up their minds that they were going to run me away also, just as they had done to my predecessors.

But I was ready for them, too. My teaching experiences in Dover had given me a positive foundation. So I knew just what to do to capture the attention and interest of my students. Without further ado, I jumped into teaching mode. My students got quiet and busy once they understood the advantage of listening, following instructions, and participating. I had the situation under control.

Professor Emerita

In the fall of 1985, my cousin, Miss Ione Vinson, called me at home in Trenton and told me that she was quite ill and was confined to her bed. She needed my help. In response to Ione's call, I took a sabbatical leave from The College of New Jersey, and went to Wilson's Mills, North Carolina, where I spent two months caring for Ione and assisting her on the road to good health.

I would like to think this kind of compassionate concern for others was evident throughout my teaching career at The College of New Jersey and was a reason that Emerita status was conferred on me. My name was submitted to the Board of Trustees of the college by my Department of Educational Administration and Secondary Education for the prestigious honor. Twenty other names were submitted from other areas/departments of the college. The responses from many of my former students and colleagues alike, were most gratifying. Along with nine other retired faculty members, I received the honor of Professor Emerita of The College of New Jersey in 1996.

An Emeritus Professor is a retired professor who has served the college and/or university with honor and distinction. This honor confers upon the recipient the rank and status enjoyed prior to retirement. The distinction is honored nationally and internationally.

I worked at The College of New Jersey for 21 years. I was in the Department of Education Administration/Secondary Education, School of Education. Dr. Richard Farber, chair of this Department, along with the other members, strongly suggested that the following information having to do with my college responsibilities as well as my community involvement be included in this writing. It is herein submitted.

Looking Back on My Career

My Teaching (Lead) Responsibilities

I taught competency-based teacher education theory and executed the practical application of that theory to all undergraduate secondary education major juniors, and supervised them as juniors and seniors in the states of New Jersey, Pennsylvania and occasionally, Delaware.

On the graduate level, the Master Degree level, I taught the required course, "Curriculum Development in the Urban/Suburban Schools," in the evenings and for six weeks of summer school. Here, I also taught, with my department colleagues, theory of competency-based teacher education and its practical application in a supervised school setting.

My College Community Responsibilities

The following are a few examples of the committees on which I served.

- The College Senate (I was a Senator);
- The Promotion Committee;
- The Academic Affairs Committee;
- The Search Committee (looking for qualified faculty to serve the college); and
- The Minority Council (lifting up the concerns and affairs of minority students).

In 1971, when I joined the faculty at the college, there were few minority professors, and I became the second female professor.

I helped to blaze paths which may be followed in the fight against racial problems and absence of females at the college.

I taught and trained students who have become outstanding teachers by demonstrating my knowledge of subject matter, demanding excellence from my students, and being honest and fair to them.

I was in my classes every day and on time, and would not tolerate absences or lateness by my students. When I retired, I had nearly 400 days in unused sick time.

Greater Trenton Community Involvement

My community involvement is very extensive. It includes membership on seven boards of directors or trustees, church choir soloist, and the founding of a community-based organization called Community Education Advisory Council (CEAC). This organization (detailed earlier in the book) works with parents, teachers and school administration to help keep all children, especially minority children, in school.

I have been praised for my speech writing and the manner in which I deliver an address. On some occasions I represented my department and the School of Education.

And, finally, I am the recipient of over 65 awards and plaques which show respect and appreciation to me for being "just Elsie. "

Living Excitingly in Retirement

When the year 1990 rolled around, I was so thoroughly involved in various activities that I had not taken the time to mentally prepare for retirement. Certain state requirements, such as pension information and review, updating of social security forms, insurance and medical forms were being taken care of, but I had not fully internalized these requirements as preparatory steps for retirement. My involvement in my work as Associate Professor at the College of New Jersey, my continued contact with and supervision of my daughters, my extensive community work on CEAC, the several boards on which I served, plus my church involvement did not provide time for me to fully examine retirement and what it would mean. Therefore, when retirement came, it was accepted as another phase in my very busy life.

When school opened in the fall of 1990, instead of greeting my incoming class of juniors and seniors at the College, as I had for two decades, Leslie and I took off for a vacation in Quebec. I spent the weekend with Leslie in New York to prepare for our two-week stay in Canada. We rented a car and drove, spending a week in Quebec City and a week in Montreal, before returning to New York.

After a few months into retirement, I was bored. My motivated mind and anxious spirit were crying out for activity and challenges which led me to search for fulfillment.

One vacation was an Amtrak trip across the country to visit my niece, Charlotte, in Seattle, Washington. A two-week stay with Charlotte was enjoyable, surpassed only by a grand tour of America.

I had spent almost 50 years in the classroom and in education administration in the eastern half of the United States. I had never crossed the country, nor seen the western coast. However, as a history/geography teacher, I had described it as accurately as I could. Now, I saw it, which gave me great pleasure. America's great mountains, valleys, hills, rivers, fields, forests, cities and resources gave me a great deal of pleasure and motivated me to take several similar trips throughout the United States.

I also made several trips to Wilson's Mills, where I spent a great deal of time with Cousin Ione. Ione's health was beginning to fail her, and she was depending more and more upon me and others to conduct important business transactions for her. My involvement in Ione's affairs began in 1985 when Ione became ill with contagious tuberculosis and was confined to her home. I then took a sabbatical leave from my position at The College of New Jersey and spent several months with Ione nursing her back to good health.

Now that I was retired, I began to spend extended visits in Wilson's Mills with Ione. It was during one of these visits that Ione reminded me again about Dr. William G. Wilson's notes and his interest in writing a history of Wilson Mills. Ione, too, was filled with a love of history about Wilson's Mills. She enjoyed telling me about the "good 'ole days," when she was a kid and a young person growing up in Wilson's Mills. These stories fascinated me so much, that Ione and I agreed that these tales should become a book for everyone to read.

It was in the mid-1980's when I first received Dr. Wilson's notes, and it was also in the 1980's when Ione told me her interesting tales about Wilson's Mills. But I was not to write about Wilson's Mills for another ten years – after the death of both Dr. Wilson, 1982 and Ione, 1993. The problem was the fear such a book about Wilson's Mills would result in the town looking like a real-life Peyton Place, and that secrets and deceptions concerning personal lives in Wilson's Mills would be revealed.

I was threatened and was told that no one would be responsible for what may happen to me if I wrote a book about Wilson's Mills and its people. I was also warned by a representative of a local organization against collaborating with a "white" man (in this case it would have been one of my colleagues at the College of New Jersey who was planning to join me there in town and research and write about the geography and scientific contributions of the area). I was frightened by the threats, for I knew too well about the damage the Ku Klux Klan could do to me and Ione. So I put the project aside.

I picked up the project again in 1994, which was ten years later. The gentleman who had spoken for Ku Klux Klan had also died. Now that I was retired, writing my book would be the challenge I needed to satisfy my motivation. So early in 1995, I began my work in earnest. I asked Paul Shelly, my godson, to serve as my editor. With the two of us at work, the book was ready for the publishers in 1997. Paul's connection, know-how and experience with publications and production of printed materials convinced me that self-publishing was one way to go. I agreed and so my first book, *Smalltown Strutters*, was published September, 1997. It was very well received by all townspeople of Wilson's Mills. I was invited to attend the Annual Homecoming Service at the White Christian Disciple Church in Wilson's Mills and bring copies of my book to sell. I did so, and sold over forty-five copies of the book at $20 per copy. The book is an interesting account of the history of the town of Wilson's Mills, plus short stories about some of its interesting and popular citizens, whom I called Strutters. Some of the tales are funny and some of them are sad, but all of them are true and quite interesting.

A couple of years later, I had an interesting conversation with Turner Vinson of Clayton, North Carolina about the book. Turner seemed a bit jealous when he explained to me that his family was in Wilson's Mills and Johnston County long before the Wilson's, who founded Wilson's Mills. He said that he had proof and would be willing to share it with me. Subsequently, he gave me volumes of materials about the Vinson family that dated as far back as 1610. With this material, along with my in-depth research on slavery in the United States and the connection my grandfather's family name of Vinson had to the "white" Vinson family name some ideas fell into place. I began to write the story. The research brought positive results. With this information, plus chats and conversations with additional Strutters, I completed my second book in 2002. It is a sequel to the first book, entitled, *Gentle People from a Not-So-Gentle Past*. My plans were to write one more book before turning my motivation to a different type of project. This book would be a personal memoir. I finally decided to take on this project because of encouragement to do so from so many people. It seems that my ability to lead a successful and satisfying life, in spite of so many heartbreaking obstacles, is worth trying to understand and explain. I believe that most people have the ability to rise above obstacles and reach their goals. What they need is the right push along, a few kind friends and mentors, and inner stick-to-it-iveness – all of this plus internal motivation.

My involvement as a community activist did not go unnoticed. The members of CEAC (Community Educational Advisory Council) decided to give me a retirement banquet. The original plan was to make it a surprise, but because of the need to involve so many people in so many different organizations and situations, it would be too difficult to keep the banquet a secret. Therefore, I was told about the banquet and I offered my cooperation in support when and where needed.

The banquet, held at the Masonic Temple in downtown Trenton, was a huge success. My dear friend and fellow Christian, Brenda Cusack chaired the event. The program was thoughtfully planned so that it would include representatives of as many aspects of my life as possible. The mayors of both Trenton and Hamilton gave remarks. There were also friends from the College of New Jersey, Educational Testing Service (ETS) of Princeton, St. Paul United Methodist Church, Alpha Kappa Alpha Sorority, Boards of Directors on which I am a member, and the community at large. Leslie and Kimberly played very prominent roles on the program, as did Paul Shelly. My brief remarks expressed my gratitude to all my friends for expressions of love and respect.

Because of my expertise in so many aspects of education, and my academic training to the level of three degrees, I was invited to serve as a consultant at Trenton Central High School. My job was to work with new and inexperienced teachers, and also, with ineffective teachers, helping to identify them. I hesitated to do so, primarily because I did not wish to become responsible to a position which would interfere with my freedom of movement and travel, and secondly, the earned money might interfere with my pension and social security benefits.

However, in the fall of 2000, I did accept the position as consultant. I served in this capacity until early November, when I entered the hospital for major surgery. I now do voluntary consulting when and where needed, if available.

I learned about the availability of a house in Smithfield, North Carolina in 1988. At no time before that was I interested in buying a house in the South. I already owned a two-bedroom co-op apartment in Trenton and a two-bedroom home in Dover, Delaware. My plans were to live in Trenton during my retirement years. Both of my daughters were married and lived quite comfortably in other states. The apartment was large enough and quite comfortable for me.

But the opportunity to buy a lovely house in Smithfield was appealing, especially since the gentleman who owned it kept coming down on its price. Also, Ione was ailing, and I needed to be nearer to her in case of sudden concerns. So, I purchased the house. It is located in an upscale neighborhood in downtown Smithfield. I immediately turned it over to the real estate agency that sold it to me, as a rental. When Ione's health began to decline, I decided to move into the house in Smithfield to be near Ione. I was given Power of Attorney over Ione's affairs and needed to be on task. In 1992, I moved into my home in Smithfield, and became the chief supervisor of the health and medical care of Ione. Ione passed away October 1993, following a massive stroke.

Several years before the serious illness, which later contributed to her death, Ione was finally able to involve me in a conversation about her property and her Will. I was reluctant, but Ione was persistent as there were several requests she wished to make certain they would be carried out. First, she asked me to take over the execution of her affairs after she passed away. She also asked me if I would carry on the management of her affairs in the event that she was unable to do so. I accepted these dual responsibilities: power of attorney and administrix of her estate. We signed the needed documents, and Ione was very appreciative.

Throughout Ione's several months of illness in 1992, I arranged for a well coordinated, around-the-clock, home healthcare system for a 24-hour time span. Three shifts of home healthcare workers came to Ione's home and cared for her. In addition, a registered nurse, as part of the medical team set up by Ione's doctor, supervised the dispensing of medicine and care for Ione. I coordinated these efforts and also paid all bills, as well. When Ione's condition worsened, she was hospitalized at Wake Medical Center, in east Raleigh.

Following two weeks in the hospital, the doctors sent Ione to a nearby nursing home for professional care. The stroke she suffered while in the hospital left her unable to speak or care for herself. I pleaded with doctors to allow me to bring Ione home in Wilson's Mills, but the doctors would not allow it because of the special techniques they were using to both feed and medicate her. There were special tubes inserted in her stomach for these procedures, which had to be monitored 24 hours a day by a registered nurse. Reluctantly, I followed the doctor's requirements and left Ione in the nursing home.

A stay at the nursing home was definitely against Ione's wishes. I had promised her faithfully that I would not send her to one, and would make sure she stayed in her own room. However, because of the need for medical supervision, I reluctantly allowed Ione to be placed in a nursing home on the grounds of a hospital. She passed away on October 17, 1993 following a brief stay of one and a half weeks at the nursing home. She was 93 years old.

Ione was a devout Jehovah's Witness. She embraced this denomination sometime during the last 20 years of her life. Throughout her youth and adult years, she was a Baptist. Her participation in the requirements of the Jehovah's Witness religious faith was as close to perfect as she could make it. As well, she also took the opportunity to convert others who were outside of the faith to join her. She was patient, but also persistent in this endeavor. She and I had an understanding in this regard. We would not allow the topic of religion to become a major issue between us. I was a Methodist and she was a Jehovah's Witness. Period.

With these thoughts in mind, I had to work with the representative of her faith to arrange her funeral services.

I held several phone conversations with the local Jehovah's Witness Assembly representative before he agreed to meet with me to arrange the funeral services. Seated at the kitchen table of my home in Smithfield, the gentleman and I discussed the format of the services. There were structural disagreements from the very beginning. Things I was familiar with, such as musical solos, tributes, poetry, etc., were not allowed. The family was not to march in, nor were the clergy. Most disturbing was his insistence that her casket would not be brought into the sanctuary, but remain in the hearse parked in front of Assembly Hall.

Strong opinions were expressed, and I was determined to have Ione's funeral conducted at the Methodist or Baptist Church in Wilson's Mills, if there was no cooperation from the representative. A third party from the Assembly intervened, and an agreement was reached. Some of my wishes were granted, such as community resolution, participation, and family and friends marching in and sitting together. However, Ione's casket was parked in front of the hall, and a picture of her was placed among the many flowers to represent her. I learned from the Assembly, later, that the entrance doors and aisles of the Hall were too small to accommodate caskets, which is why they were left in the hearse outside. I later expressed this information to the representative and told him that I would have understood had he been honest with me about the Hall's problem.

The funeral services of Ione went well, and were attended by many relatives and friends. I had her buried in the Richardson family plot, where my family members are buried in Wilson's Mills.

Epilogue

Well into my senior years, I enjoy my freedom of movement and decision-making privileges and accredit my successes as a human being to my ability to keep an open mind and a strong believe in Divine Power. I am not quick to jump to conclusions, but find it absolutely necessary to think through a situation and carefully examine all available aspects before drawing a conclusion. Honesty and fair play are also a must in my book. Throughout my teaching career, I found it absolutely necessary to be honest with my students and treat all of them fairly. By doing so, I would earn their respect and full cooperation.

When I was born, segregation and discrimination against non-white Americans, was the "law of the land." Non-white Americans were classified as second class citizens and were therefore expected to perform differently than members of the majority race. They were looked down upon and were, therefore, regarded as non-human or un-human. This belief was handed down in the American culture and belief system from generation to generation of the majority culture.

I battled my way through this cloud of negativism, non-acceptance, lack of equal opportunity, poverty and disrespect. There were many times when I was crushed, overwhelmed, and downright angry. But my inner faith and religious mindset enabled me to play it cool and work out strategies and approaches that would solve the problems facing me. I always believed that I was in God's presence, and that His power guided me.

I continue to serve as a volunteer to my community and fellow citizens in general. My services as a board member on the Rescue Mission of Greater Trenton were continuous since 1980 but ended in 2007 when I retired and was awarded emeritus status. I am one of the original members appointed by the County Commissioners of Johnston County, North Carolina to the Board of Commissioners of the Johnston County Heritage Center, Smithfield, North Carolina since 1997. I continuously served on the John O. Wilson Neighborhood Service Center from 1978 through 2008, and served on the Administrative Board of my church, St. Paul United Methodist Church, Trenton from 1990 until about 2005 when the church merged with another. I continue to help interested students matriculate at The College of New Jersey through my affiliation with the college and I also write several letters of recommendation per year for individuals applying to graduate schools or new jobs. I have now limited the number of addresses and speeches I deliver per year. However, in 2002, I was the speaker for the Johnson County Training School/Johnson Central High School Alumni Banquet, Smithfield, North Carolina and the Woman's Day speaker, Millers Chapel AME Zion Church, Goldsboro, North Carolina, in May 2003.

Two special events that I look forward to are as follows: the annual family reunion of the Holts-Isley-Banks Family Reunion and the William Henry Comprehensive High School Alumni Celebration every three years in Dover, Delaware. I make it my business to be in attendance to enjoy the family connections and the wonderful fellowships among many friends and former students that envelope each affair.

Another wonderful thing has happened recently. At the first meeting of the Vinson Family Retreat in 2007, I was regarded as the Family Matriarch and made chair of the Executive Planning Board. Our task is to write policy to establish the Vinson Retreat organization and determine its direction and longevity.

I am often "on the go," traveling between my two homes; one in Smithfield and the other in Trenton. Between these travels, I visit my two daughters: one now in Hamilton, New Jersey and the other in Dover, Delaware, and also keep in contact with my doctors in Virginia and New Jersey. Among the highlights of my visits is the fun I have with my grandchildren. I am known as "Mimi," and the grandchildren look forward to my visits with them and their visits to my homes.

Kissi and Mimi, Elsie and Professor Collins. I answer to all these names, for they reflect who I am, where I came from, and how far I have journeyed. I go on in life empowered by God and, as the Apostle Paul phrased it, "with a spirit of power, of love and of self-discipline."

Elsie's grandparents, Emzy and Allie Richardson.

Elsie's mother, Ruth L. McIntosh

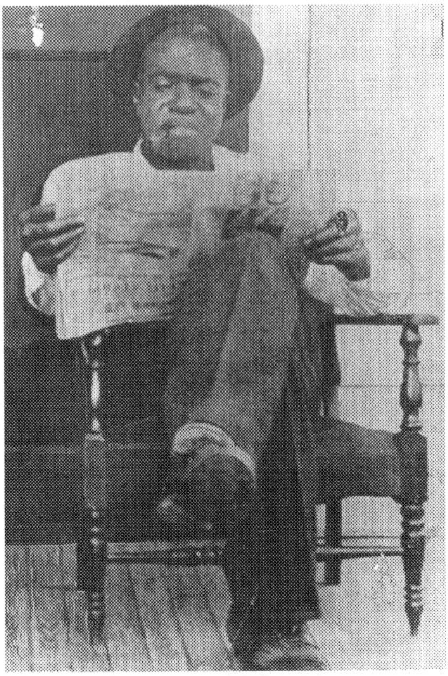

Uncle David Richardson (Elsie's mother's brother).

Elsie's great grandmother Ruthie, who lived to be 104 years old, (seated, right), her daughter Nora (left), granddaughter Melissa (standing).

Aunt Nellie R. Rodgers (Elsie's mother's sister).

The Richardsons – Uncle Purl (Elsie's mother's brother) with his wife (Aunt) Sallie and Leamon (adopted brother) age 7, in front of their home in Wilson's Mills, N.C.

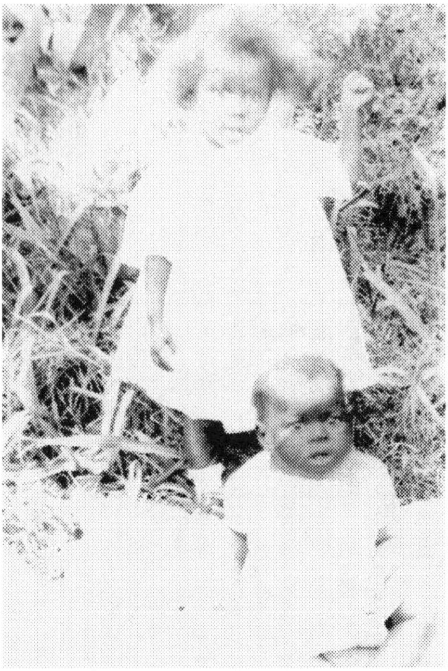

Elsie, age 2½ (standing) with sister Allie (7 months)

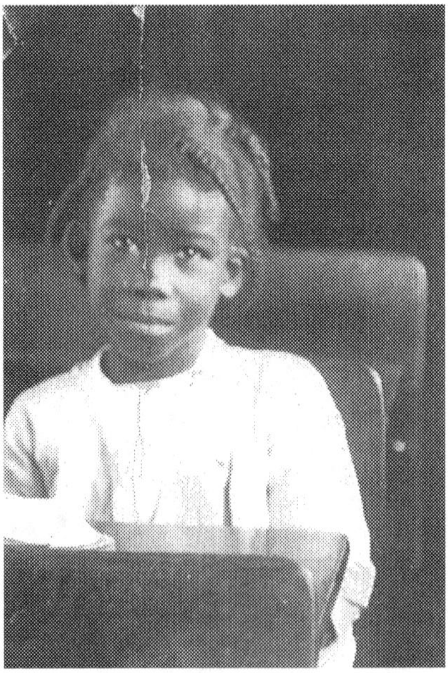

Elsie (age 6) in second grade classroom at Short Journey Elementary School for Colored Children

Elsie's teachers at Short Journey Elementary School for Colored Children, Johnston County, N.C.. Elsie traveled to school each day for seven years with Miss Ione vison (fifth from left on bottom row) and Mrs. Rachelle Vinson (third from left on top row).

Amy Barry with her daughter, Judy (left) and an unidentified child. Elsie was Judy's babysitter.

Elsie, a teenager

Elsie in her 20's, a young teacher (middle school and high school), Dover, Delaware.

Elsie and sisters at home in New York City (left to right: Elizabeth, Elsie and Allie).

Elsie with her mother-in-law, Isabelle C. Collins.

Amy and Joseph Evans with two-year-old Kimberly Ruth Collins, their godchild.

Elsie in Doctoral attire. Her educational roles included Curriculum Specialist and Professor with New York City School System and The College of New Jersey (formerly Trenton State College).

Ms. Genvieve Wisner, music professor at Delaware State College (now Delaware State University) who stimulated Elsie's interest in classical music and her training as a soloist and recitalist.

Dr. D'Arce, Elsie's French Teacher at Kittrell College, Kittrell, N.C.. Studying under him, Elsie's command of the French language enabled her to speak it fluently. It was one of her four college majors.

Elsie's daughter Leslie's family (left to right: Leslie Collins Ramsey, with husband Daniel Morgan Ramsey; and daughters Macy Grayson and Casidy Ellen-Ann Ramsey).

Kimberly's family – Aubrey, her husband and four of their children (before Amari was born). Children standing (left to right: Melody, twins Alexis and Aubrey, Jr.; and Albany, beside father)

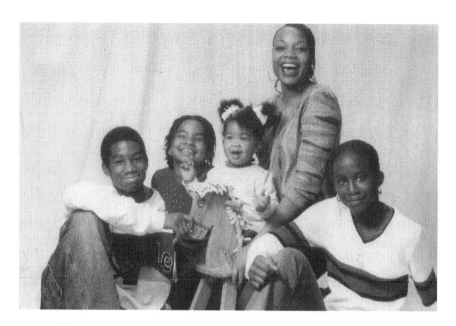

Grandchildren: Kimberly's children (left to right: Aubrey, Jr.; Albany; Amari; Melody and Alexis)

Elsie's granddaughter, Melody with great-granddaughter Harmone Lythe (shown age 1).

Elsie's "blended" grandsons (left to right: Jason L. Myers, Christopher D. Myers and Kwaine A. Myers).

Elsie and her special friend, David Fluck, MD at a business meeting in Trenton, New Jersey.

Colonel Kindrick Few (one of five sons) of Dr. William Preston Few, President of Duke University, Dunham, N.C.). Elsie's mother was the Fews' housekeeper.

Elsie in retirement, shown holding her second book Gentle People from a Not So Gentle Past *(2002). Smalltown Strutters was her first book (1997). At this time, she was Emerita Professor, The College of New Jersey.*

Elsie, now in retirement.